HOW TO THINK
LIKE A LAWYER—
AND WHY

ALSO BY KIM WEHLE

How to Read the Constitution—and Why
What You Need to Know About Voting—and Why

HOW TO THINK LIKE A LAWYER— AND WHY

A COMMON-SENSE GUIDE TO EVERYDAY DILEMMAS

KIM WEHLE

HARPER

NEW YORK • LONDON • TORONTO • SYDNEY

HARPER

FIRST EDITION

Designed by Jen Overstreet

Library of Congress Cataloging-in-Publication Data has been applied for.

ISBN 978-0-06-306756-1 (pbk.)

22 23 24 25 26   LSC   10 9 8 7 6 5 4 3 2 1

I lovingly dedicate this book to my
grandparents, Ann and Jack Nelson,
who used common sense to live with integrity.

Contents

Introduction

The straight line, a respectable optical
illusion which ruins many a man.
—Victor Hugo, *Les Misérables*

While many of the people I come across in my life are either lawyers or are planning to become lawyers (blame Washington, D.C., and the local law school where I teach), even those with established careers not in law often tell me that they wish they had gone to law school. Still, a lot of people in the world don't love lawyers. Many believe that lawyers mostly add conflict to situations, rather than diffuse them, and that we do tend to do so aggressively, arrogantly, and without compassion. Lawyers are expensive, the legal system is painfully slow, and lawyers can make an astounding amount of money—lots more than most Americans. Drive down virtually any highway in America and you'll see a billboard touting legal services for individuals who may have been in a car accident or experienced botched health care, possibly reinforcing the stereotype of lawyers as money-motivated predators willing to file bogus lawsuits that wind up burdening the rest of society in one way or another.

That said, it's often those same people who—when facing a decision about family or work or other responsibilities—find themselves suddenly considering hiring a lawyer or wishing they could somehow "think like a lawyer" to solve their problems. I hope this book will teach exactly that.

Do you need to make health care decisions for an aging parent but are unsure where to start? Are you at a crossroads in your career and don't really know how to move through it? Are you facing divorce and custody decisions and don't know how to even begin? Everyone needs to make big decisions in life, but not everyone can or will hire a lawyer. This is a book that will help you think for yourself, like a lawyer.

Anyone who is married to a lawyer or has a close friend who practices law knows that lawyers "think" a bit differently—we often argue points that maybe should be left alone or find ourselves picking up typos on restaurant menus "just because." This book won't turn you into a lawyer; there are probably enough of us already. Still, thinking like a lawyer is a valuable skill. This book will share some of those skills outside the law school classroom. While it's true that law students, lawyers, and judges study lots of cases, the reason they do it in law school is that cases help people learn some basic legal skills, which I will begin to teach you here. They include:

- How to break complex issues into pieces
- How to gather pertinent facts, expertise, and competing points of view and then exhaust possible options

- How to anticipate what the other person is going to say
- How to consider the precedents that might be set by each choice and what each means for the future
- How to identify whose interests are at stake and whose interests should be served
- How to get buy-in from people affected by an outcome in squishy gray areas
- How to accept an outcome that you, personally, might not like but will tolerate as it may be the better path overall

It turns out that making decisions based on information that we already know and believe—and aligning new experiences to our past experiences and beliefs—is a very handy and productive means of making quick calls in a pinch. If we stand in line to buy a movie ticket and find out that the show we wanted to see is sold out, we might pick a runner-up based on existing biases: our lifelong affinity for thrillers or rom-coms, for example, or the belief that anything with Meryl Streep is probably good. By relying on our own biases and past experiences, chances are that we will choose a film that satisfies.

To some degree, that kind of practical, or "heuristic," decision-making comes into play when we buy a car or even a house. We identify our likes and dislikes based on past experiences in order to sort through the options. Some people will always buy a Ford no matter what. Others might focus on gas mileage or emissions standards of various options. But because these purchases involve relatively high dollar amounts and even (at least for cars) personal safety, completely relying on our own, hard-wired notions of good and bad can be a bit risky. Unlike buying a movie ticket, the consequences of other decisions are lasting. So, in many situations we're better off looking to more sophisticated methods of decision-making rather than simply falling back on what we already know. We might gather additional facts about car options, read opinions reviewing various cars, and maybe even speak to friends who recently purchased a car and piggyback on what they learned through the car-buying process.

Much of our decision-making methodology is automatic—even unconscious. But there exists a host of scholarly, scientific, and business-oriented resources about how to make good decisions more deliberately. Corporations will, and do, pay large amounts of dollars to consultants to better train their workforces around decision-making. And, of course, there are lawyers. Many people assume that lawyers become involved in decision-making only when there are laws involved, because lawyers—unlike the rest of the population—know something about the law. Like a doctor who has studied medicine and understands how the body works and its reaction to various interventions, lawyers know how to discern what the Constitution, statutes, regulations, and judicial decisions say. They are called upon to translate that language in ways that make sense to clients.

But describing the law is only a small part of how lawyers add value for their individual clients and society at large. Lawyers know how to think and make decisions in ways that non-lawyers generally don't. Law students learn *how* to think through thorny problems—not *what* to think. I have seen it happen with hundreds of students during their first year of law school. And lawyering is a relatively unique skill. Gaming experts who have programmed computers to simulate medical exams have told me that simulating legal analysis is much more complex and nuanced, if doable at all. The value of a lawyerly mind is not something, at least for now, that artificial intelligence has successfully imitated.

Think about what happens when you visit a doctor. Medical professionals match symptoms against their vast knowledge base and make predictions and diagnoses based on how a patient's symptoms and lab work match up with the characteristics of a particular medical condition. Good doctors and nurses are good communicators who know how to ask the right questions of a patient—and how to listen to their patients' experiences and needs. They are organized, compassionate, and conscientious. All of these skills can be brought to bear on good lawyering too.

Medical students are usually taught some form of diagnostic process—assessment, testing, treatment, referral, and follow-up. Based on that information, they formulate a decision tree. The trunk of the tree might be a patient's primary symptom, with arrows leading to other secondary symptoms and "yes" or "no" questions about whether, for example, the patient has a fever or not. Computer scientists have managed to develop algorithms that simulate the process of medical diagnosis.

Lawyers work from facts and precedents too, but legal decision-making especially benefits from independent and creative thinking. Law students may need to memorize information for certain exams, but lawyers can't just regurgitate Wikipedia entries to address their clients' problems, nor do they just look up legal rules and tell clients what the rules say. Skilled lawyers crave ambiguity and nuance. They look for the nooks and crannies of a problem that has no clear answers and craft a series of possible responses or approaches. It's an entirely different way of thinking than jumping to a conclusion or a "side" and finding arguments to support a preconceived point of view. Even when lawyers are tasked with advocating a position vigorously for a client, part of their preparation is to exhaust all opposing arguments. Black-and-white thinking is very risky for lawyers because they can miss something important—and lose a case, a client, or even a bar license as a result.

In my law school classes, I often call on students randomly and fire off questions—an event that can be stressful for some on the receiving end. When a student stumbles, I might rephrase the question with the instruction, "just use your logical mind." Detached from legal formalities, students inevitably reason through tricky issues using their life experiences, their values, the information provided, and their common sense. So, in this book, I will also draw on the human capacity for common sense.

An Opening Hypothetical

Let's start our conversation—as I often do in law school classrooms—with a hypothetical. Imagine that you book a weekend trip to Las Vegas through a last-minute internet pop-up ad. Round-trip airfare for one from anywhere in the United States, two nights in a four-star hotel, and a luxury welcome package— all for $399.99! You arrive there but the hotel is overbooked, so you have to wait several hours for a room. The room that the hotel—let's call it Hotel Ooh La La—assigns you has just been painted so it smells toxic, and it's situated on the first floor next to the parking lot exit that opens to a block of stinky dumpsters. The hallway is extremely noisy, because it's Spring Break (pre-coronavirus), and partygoers are dragging cases of beer from the parking lot down the hall. The "welcome package" turns out to be a bottle of fake apple cider champagne and a mandatory "invitation" to sit through a ninety-minute lecture about timeshare opportunities as a precondition to securing the reduced occupancy rate. You decide to grab a real drink at the pool bar first. On your way past the pool, you spy a woman in a bathing suit that looks like it's made of python-printed fabric. The suit turns out to be a live python. Startled, you slip, fall, and break your ankle. What do you do?

When I give this hypothetical to first-year law students, the virtually universal, reflexive response is: "Sue Hotel Ooh La La." Perhaps this reflex comes from the knowledge that it's law school, and lawyers have a reputation for suing everyone. But there's probably more to this instinct. We are all well-acquainted with making snap judgments in the moment because life often calls on us to do so. And a lot of the time, we're smart to trust those instincts. But in law, methodical, careful, and thorough analysis is the touchstone of decision-making. Often, it's a judge or a client who actually makes the decision—but it's the lawyers who present the various issues and wrinkles lurking underneath a bigger decision in the first place.

It turns out that there's a trove of scientific literature on how people make decisions. But there's relatively scant literature out there about what makes legal analysis different from other modes of decision-making. But before we get there, let's look at some of the existing research on decision-making.

Making good decisions is a critical component to having a happy and fulfilling life. We make decisions every day—some big and complicated, some small and unnoticed. How we make decisions is a topic that spans mathematics, sociology, psychology, economics, political science, philosophy, and even religion. It's fascinating.

Only a few hundred years ago, until around the seventeenth century, people relied primarily on hope, faith, and guesswork to make decisions. Mostly, they believed they had little control over life events, instead using priests and oracles to predict the future. Mathematical models for making predictions were either non-existent or clumsy. It wasn't until the advent of our current Hindu-Arabic numeric system that the number zero even existed. The number system began in India in the sixth or seventh century and spread through Europe around the twelfth century. Then, in the sixteenth century, a Swiss scholar named Daniel Bernoulli spearheaded the use of numbers (let's call it "mathematics") for managing risk. To this day, we refer to ways of limiting our exposure to potential losses in the future as "hedging our bets," which is a nod to Bernoulli's spadework.

Decision-making theory really picked up in the twentieth century. After World War II, the U.S. government initiated a campaign to get consumers to eat more organ meat. They enlisted the help of a psychologist named Kurt Lewin who found that people were more likely to eat differently if they talked through the subject with other people; lecturing others about food didn't do much. His discovery is known as "field theory," and it established the common-sense notion that people are influenced by other people when they make decisions, even if they start out with very different goals or perspectives.

In the 1950s, a psychologist named Solomon Asch conducted a series of experiments, in which he put eight people in a room and showed them a series of vertical lines. Seven of the individuals worked for Asch. Only one was a real experimental participant, and that person was led to believe the others were too. Each person was asked to state out loud which comparison line (A, B, or C) was most like the target line.

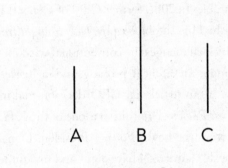

Target Line   Comparison Lines

The real participant was always asked the question last. In a total of eighteen trials, when the seven "stooges" gave an incorrect answer, the real participant conformed to the majority view twelve times. In other words, even though the correct answer was obviously C, around 75% of participants succumbed to group pressure and gave the wrong answer. Only 25% of participants declined to conform to the group.

In 1972, a man named Irving Janis coined the term "group-think" to describe this kind of team decision-making, which is done hastily and without questioning basic assumptions. Group-think occurs when a group's desire to agree overrides the need to explore important alternatives.

Gut Decisions

Of course, some decisions are best made by following instincts—a gut feeling that something is or is not the right thing to do. That way of thinking may even be considered courageous—and thus admirable. In 2001, former CEO of General Electric Jack Welch published his autobiography, *Jack: Straight from the Gut*, the title of which challenges the conventional wisdom that good decision-making is methodical, probing, and inclusive. As Alden Hayashi wrote in an article on CEO decision-making for the *Harvard Business Review*, "[i]ntuition is one of the X factors separating the men from the boys." Former President Donald Trump likewise famously claimed, "I have a gut and my gut tells me more sometimes than anybody else's brain can ever tell me."

Gut decision-making is necessary if a crisis of the moment requires it. Once, on my commute from Washington, D.C., to Baltimore, M.D., on Interstate 95, I was driving behind a car in the middle lane of a three-lane highway going 65 miles per hour. The car in front of me slammed on the brakes. In less time than it would have taken me to look over my left or right shoulder to see if it was safe to merge into the next lane and avoid a collision, a voice inside my head went through a fairly complex decision-making process. In what felt like a blink of an eye, I concluded that I could merge either left or right but that there was no telling whether either choice was safe. I then determined that I am more confident in my merging skills if I move right than if I merge left. I thus calculated that the manageable risk was less if I merged right than if I merged left, even if the unmanageable risk (whether I'd hit a car in either direction) was beyond my control. I merged right. There was no car there, so I got lucky. I then burst into tears from the adrenaline and stress.

Gut decisions are crucial to the human species' survival. Sometimes, a gut decision—like getting sucked into click-bait that produces a useless trinket on your doorstep for the great price of $39.99—is not a good thing, at least in hindsight. But people admire gut decision-making as courageous and reflective of confidence. Gut decisions are often made with scant information and little precedent. Howard Shultz took a risk in charging Americans a whopping $3 for a cup of coffee, and Starbucks made history. George Soros made more than $39 billion in hedge funds by purportedly relying on what he called his "animal instincts" as well as (somewhat bizarrely) the state of his physical "back pain."

One way of organizing gut decision-making processes is around a set of strategies called "heuristics." Heuristics are mental shortcuts that people use to make decisions with little information. Here are some examples:

- The **price heuristic** assumes that higher-priced items are of better quality than lower-priced ones.
- The **outrage heuristic** tempts people to determine punishment based on how horrible a crime seems.

- The **highly researched heuristic** suggests that people are likely to focus on information that they already know—an idea that could affect medical professionals as they make diagnoses.
- The **anchoring and adjustment heuristics** appear in negotiations. A couple purchasing a new home will adjust the home's value based on the original number provided at the start of the negotiations—even if the actual value of the property is far different.
- The **anticipated regret heuristic** tracks how we make decisions to avoid regret later. People are willing to pay extra for the option of changing their minds after the fact, although the ability to reverse a decision can actually make it harder to feel good about it.
- The **elimination by aspects heuristic** describes how people eliminate options that don't meet a minimum cut-off for attributes that especially matter to that person. Through a process of elimination, people then cross off options with the next lowest value until a single choice remains.

Research shows that heuristics can produce effective, accurate decision-making but that no single heuristic works for all situations. Decisions that need a high level of accuracy require more complex and deliberate thinking.

Researchers have also categorized innate ways of decision-making into several so-called cognitive biases, which can sometimes lead to memory errors, faulty logic, and bad judgment. Here are a few of them:

- **Belief Bias.** Belief bias is our tendency to rely on prior beliefs rather than logic in making decisions. If a conclusion aligns with a belief system, we might ignore the specifics and focus on the outcome. This happens a lot in politics. A strongly held belief that immigration hurts the economy, for example, could lead a person to oppose any reform that could increase immigration—regardless of the merits of the reform or its positive impact on the economy or immigrant families.

- **Hindsight Bias.** Hindsight bias is the tendency to overestimate the ability to have predicted an outcome after the fact. Imagine, for example, that you are going on a long car ride, and you wind up leaving thirty minutes later than you planned. You hit bad traffic, and exclaim, "I knew this would happen. We should have left earlier!"

- **Omission Bias.** Omission bias (also called "status-quo" bias) is the tendency to skip over information that feels risky or induces anxiety, and thus to favor inaction over action. Inaction is viewed as less blameworthy. Telling a lie (an action) is considered worse than withholding the truth (an omission), for example.

- **Confirmation Bias.** Confirmation bias is the tendency for people to pick out what they already expect to find in making observations. Imagine that a person believes that left-handed people are more creative than right-handed people. Whenever that person witnesses a left-handed person displaying creativity, they will credit this as "evidence" of their bias. They might even seek out more proof to back up this belief—and discount the evidence of creativity on the part of right-handed people.

- **Escalation of Commitment.** People tend to invest more and more time, money, and effort into a decision that they've already committed to. Imagine a family-owned restaurant that decides to open for breakfast as well as lunch and dinner. The owners add morning shifts, a breakfast menu, and sidewalk signs to lure people in. When the breakfast traffic doesn't catch on, they decide to spend more money on digital advertising of the breakfast menu and 10%-off breakfast coupons. In the end, good money is wasted. People make risky decisions when they feel they've already sunk time, money, and effort into a project—or that they are already too far "in the hole" to dig out.

A big reason why humans toggle between considered, logical analysis and gut decision-making is brain chemistry. Most of our decision-making is unconscious, as our brains process approximately 11,000,000 pieces of data each second. The front part of the brain contains what's known as the "vetromedial prefrontal cortex" or "vmPFC." The vmPFC helps regulate fear by stopping an individual from being afraid in certain situations. By contrast, the amygdala—an almond-shaped structure in the center of each brain hemisphere—prepares the body to respond to threats. It reacts to fear with "fight" or "flight."

So, if you are feeling anxious about making a decision, having someone persuade you that an action is the right way to go could trigger your vmPFC, allowing you to make a decision that is less induced by fear, but doesn't necessarily weigh the practical pros and cons of the choice. When the brain decides to be confident about a decision, there is a neuron that fires and prompts you to act regardless of the downsides.

But there's more. Value-based decisions (like buying a Subaru instead of a Volvo) are made in what's called the orbitofrontal cortex, or OFC. However, habit-based decisions (like pulling your favorite cereal off the grocery store shelf) are made in the basal ganglia. The basal ganglia only kick in when the OFC is inactive, which suggests that we cannot make decisions based on habit *and* value at the same time. If the brain is presented with a lot of information, the basal ganglia—which form the habit-based decision center of the brain—become quiet, and the OFC takes over by assessing the issue based on relative value.

Complex Decisions

A significant body of literature also exists around problem-solving strategies for complex decisions. We have all heard of things like brainstorming, identifying goals, and drafting "pros and cons" lists. In evaluating a decision entailing some complexity, we might identify what things are important to us, assess the feasibility of each of those attributes actually coming to fruition, and then decide which attributes we're willing to forgo in favor of one or more of the others.

Think about the last time you decided to go on vacation. You might care a lot about warm weather, a non-touristy environment, and a relatively short flight. The availability of water sports or whether the English language is widely spoken at the various destination options might not matter much to you. Moreover, some attributes are certain—like the language spoken—whereas others are not. Weather is notoriously in the latter category. You can book a Caribbean vacation only to arrive for a week of rain. Some people are more thorough than others in considering all relevant information, but all of us are ultimately willing to accept the loss of one attribute to gain another when it comes to choosing a vacation destination.

Legal analysis falls under the complex decision-making category, for sure. But it is also framed by procedural systems that impose requirements aimed at getting decisions by judges and juries that are fair, accurate, and efficient. Consider again the Hotel Ooh La La hypothetical. Suing Hotel Ooh La La over a slip-and-fall at the pool would thrust the dispute into the judicial system. A judge will decide things like what kind of facts each side can discover from the other side—such as what witnesses, documents, medical reports, and even what video evidence must be turned over. The court will also decide whether the case is worth bringing to a jury at all—an inquiry that boils down to asking whether there are enough facts backing up both sides of the story to even bother a jury with deciding which party should win.

If a case does go to trial, the judge will apply strict rules of evidence to make sure that nothing unreliable, biased, or fake goes before the jury. The judge will also instruct the jury on the law—in this case, the law of negligence—so that the jury knows which precise factual issues are important enough so that, if the injured hotel guest proves those facts, it will allow them to get a court order directing that the hotel turn over some money to address their injuries.

When we see big disputes of national concern play out in the media or among politicians, it's important to bear in mind that the facts each side relies on to support its respective arguments are *not* put through the filter of the judicial system. As viewers, we need to apply our own rules of "evidence" to determine what kind of information goes into our brains for purposes of making important decisions. The same goes for our daily lives—when we make important decisions, we need to start with good information.

Even if the Hotel Ooh La La dispute were to resolve short of a lawsuit—by, say, the injured customer asking the hotel to willingly provide compensation, or by going to a mediator who can help the parties reach a solution—the same foundational tenets of good decision-making will come into play. Good facts are absolutely essential to good decisions.

Law students struggle mightily to master the basics of thinking like a lawyer. In this book, I hope you will find a few ideas that will help you think differently—and perhaps better—about hard problems in your own life too. Each chapter discusses a category of decisions that many people make at some point or another in their lives—such as divorce and custody, civic participation, health care, and work life—and unveils how a lawyer's mind might approach them to make a decision that's methodical and informed, rather than reactive.

As the book unfolds, I will reveal what I call a lawyer's "framework" for decision-making. The framework has the following components, which we will return to in each chapter, along with checklists that can be used in everyday decision-making. The framework has five steps, which I call the B-I-C-A-T method:

1. **Break** the problem down.
2. **Identify** your values and your aim.
3. **Collect** lots of knowledge.
4. **Argue** both sides of each point.
5. **Tolerate** the fact that people will disagree with your choice—and that you might feel conflicted.

The book will wrap up with a discussion of the kinds of life circumstances in which you might actually need to hire a lawyer and how to find the right one for you and the particular problem you are facing. Not all lawyers are the same. Not all are even competent. But when you need one, you need one. The skills I discuss in this book will help you with that too.

HOW TO THINK
LIKE A LAWYER—
AND WHY

1

Thinking Like a
Lawyer at Work

Start by doing what's necessary, then do what's possible;
and suddenly you are doing the impossible.
—Saint Francis

It has happened to all of us. You're exhausted after a long day or week or month of work, you've been a little on edge, haven't slept, and maybe fought with your kids before work. Suddenly, around 4 p.m., just as your mood is at its lowest, you get an email. @#$%&*, it says (fill in the blank—it's not pretty). It's from your WHAT? Boss? Co-worker?

For many of us, the immediate response to the nastygram might be one that we ultimately regret—a reactive email that displays hurt or anger but doesn't implement a strategy for solving the underlying problem. As we saw in the introduction to this book, our brains are wired to react to stress and potential danger. Often, reactivity can be an excellent way to resolve a problem. But reactivity in the workplace—much like in our closest relationships outside of work—can cause problems for you later. There are often better ways, and taking a breather before pressing send is a critical habit to develop.

The importance of pausing before reacting at work cannot be overstated. When faced with an immediate stressor—like I was on the highway that day—your body responds with a series of automatic chemical and physical reactions. A tiny region at the base of your brain called the hypothalamus prompts your adrenal glands—which sit on top of your kidneys—to release powerful hormones, including adrenaline and cortisol. Adrenaline increases your heart rate and your blood pressure. Cortisol causes glucose—or sugar—to surge in the bloodstream and enter your brain. Cortisol also boosts other substances in your body that function to repair tissues, while slowing down bodily functions that are non-essential to a fight-or-flight response, like the digestive and reproductive organs.

In a normal day, your body releases cortisol in the morning, waking you up for the day. Levels decrease as you wind down toward the evening. But in a stressful situation, cortisol levels surge within about fifteen minutes and can remain elevated for hours. Your breathing rate also increases, you get sweaty, and your pupils dilate—the telltale signs of a state of anxiety. Keep in mind that your body does this because it perceives a physical or psychological threat to your safety. After millennia of evolutionary development, your brain understands that the danger is likely unpredictable and could even be uncontrollable. You are on high alert for reasons that might have very little to do with the actual contents of the snarky email.

If you are in a position to wait a day or so before responding to the email, do it. But if the email is time-sensitive, give yourself at least thirty minutes before hitting send so that the stress hormones have a chance to subside, putting your brain function closer to its normal or resting state. If responding with "I'll get back to you later today" makes you feel a little better while your body adjusts, do that. But avoid making significant decisions about your work life while in a state of physiological stress or even panic.

With that tip out of the way, this chapter explains and applies the first step in the lawyering framework to the workplace: breaking the problem down. This is an absolutely foundational and essential aspect of lawyering, which I often refer to as the "no glomming" rule to my students. To "glom" means to become stuck or attached to something else. When problems or issues are all glommed together into one big wad of confusion, it's very hard to address the questions individually, and important nuances get lost. For lawyers, those nuances can make all the difference in the outcome of a case, as I will illustrate.

But for starters, let's run through a few basic caveats. Workplace psychology is a deep and expansive field. My alma mater, Cornell University, has an entire undergraduate school devoted to learning about labor relations. There's lots of expertise out there around workplace decision-making, too. For an employee, many factors come into play in making a job-related choice, including the individuals' job preferences and attitudes, age, education levels, locale, socio-economic and racial diversity, digital skills, personality factors, work-family balance, work overload, work underload, bad bosses, monotony, stress-reduction skills,

pay, promotion opportunities, benefits, schedules, physical haz-
ards, ethnic and gender discrimination or harassment, telecommuting challenges, on-site working conditions, commute, access
to unions, governing personnel rules and policies, and the organizational culture.

For employers, things like organizational management,
employee engagement, workday schedules, benefits and other
incentivization structures, training, feedback, union influence,
organizational culture, team behavior, cyberslacking and mon-
itoring, conflict resolution procedures, part-time employment
options, profit and loss management, and hiring and firing criteria are all critical to an organization's success. A comprehensive
or deep dive into any of these topics is beyond the scope of this
book. But lawyering skills can be brought to bear in virtually any
workplace setting—and readily so.

Here, again, is the five-step B-I-C-A-T framework:

1. **Break** the problem down.
2. **Identify** your values and your aim.
3. **Collect** lots of knowledge.
4. **Argue** both sides of each point.
5. **Tolerate** the fact that people will disagree with your
   choice—and that you might feel conflicted.

In this chapter, we will focus on **Step 1: Break the problem
down.** As a longtime law professor, I cannot help but approach
the subject of thinking like a lawyer with the predominant tool
that has had students quaking in law-school classrooms for cen-

turies: the case method. Instead of reading a bunch of rules, law professors have students read court decisions in which judges applied rules to a particular dispute between a plaintiff and a defendant. The dispute is one that has never appeared before that court in the exact same way. So, the court's job is to compare and contrast that case with the ones that came before it and decide which is closest to the one the court must decide. If the earlier case had the plaintiff winning, then the court might rule for the plaintiff in the most recent case. If the defendant won in the most analogous case, then the defendant might win this time too.

A lawyer's job is to identify the outcome they want for the client; for example, a plaintiff's lawyer will want a win for the plaintiff. The lawyer will try to find a prior decision in which a plaintiff already won on a similar issue, and then argue "me too!" before the judge. In other words, the lawyer will aim to convince the judge that the present case is just like that prior case. The defendant's lawyer, by contrast, will want to distinguish that case—to argue "not it!"—and persuade the judge that the case now before the court is different from the older one in which the defendant lost.

Sometimes, the law governing the case is in a statute or even the Constitution itself. Sometimes, the law is threaded among a bunch of prior cases, and it's hard to identify what the rule is. Teaching students to reconcile cases that seem to go in opposite directions is one of the tasks of a law professor. It still ultimately comes down to "me too!" or "not it!" Helping students get into a habit of drawing analogies to older cases—

rather than jumping to a conclusion as to the "right" answer in a new case based on their own instincts of fairness—is perhaps my most important objective as a teacher during students' first year of law school.

But another task of a law professor is teaching students how to read the cases in the first place. Cases—or opinions written by judges resolving a dispute—can be really confusing. I recall being a first-year student in a course called "Property." It took me about five hours to read a case that was only a few pages long, because it was hundreds of years old, used an arcane version of the English language, and contained so many wonky legal terms and procedural references that my head was swimming. I eventually learned that lawyers need to spend time at the beginning of a case just getting their bearings. Otherwise, it can feel like trying to complete a jigsaw puzzle with only a handful of pieces and no picture of the finished product on the puzzle box for guidance.

One way that lawyers get their bearings is to break the problem apart into pieces, and then break those pieces into even smaller pieces. Once the issues and sub-issues are on the table (much like a jigsaw puzzle with all its pieces), the lawyer can begin to work through them one by one. Breaking the problem up into smaller pieces also allows the lawyer to identify what I call the "heart" of the case—the key question or objective—and to prioritize the rest. Doing this with big problems in everyday life can also help you get your bearings and start to tackle each piece with diligence.

Let's apply Step 1 of the framework through an actual case that every lawyer and law student in America has probably read—and struggled with—at some point in law school. (And yes, the case reviews throughout this book would come in handy for your friend or family member who is about to begin law school.)

First, an explanatory note: If you find that the case discussions feel bogged down, you can skip ahead, of course. But just as law students cannot learn the skill of breaking things down simply by being told to "break things down," readers of this book can't learn how to think like a lawyer simply by being told what to do. Law students learn the skills through the case method, so I'm going to use that teaching technique here too. It's like riding a bike: I can tell my child twice a week for seventy-five minutes each time over thirteen weeks how to ride a bike. I can explain that you put one leg over the bike, balance on the seat, put your dominant foot on a pedal and start pushing the wheel, and then try to steer it so it holds steady. But she still won't learn how to ride the bike. She won't learn until she gets on the bike, wobbles, and falls a few times. Thinking like a lawyer works the same way. The cases are included in this book to help get you on that bike. There's no way through the thicket of learning these new skills other than by actually seeing how the skills are used by lawyers and judges, and then actually using them, until it becomes second nature.

A Law School Lesson: *Pennoyer v. Neff*

How Do Lawyers—and Judges—Break a
Complex Dispute into Bite-Sized Pieces?

To be honest, anyone who has been to law school might groan at the mention of *Pennoyer v. Neff*, a U.S. Supreme Court case from 1878 involving a concept known as "personal jurisdiction." Personal jurisdiction is about the power of a court to issue a judgment against a defendant, forcing the defendant to pay money or act in a certain way. Courts have powers that regular people do not. If a court orders that you pay money and you refuse, it can order a sheriff to come take steps to wrest the money from you. If I take steps to take money from you, it's stealing. So personal jurisdiction protects defendants against an *unfair* use of the vast power of a court.

If I'm sued in Hawaii but live in Washington, D.C., and the Hawaii court issues an order forcing me to pay money to a plaintiff, is that fair? After all, I've never even been to Hawaii. How can it be fair that I must trek there to defend myself in a lawsuit (as lovely as its beaches are)? If both parties are from Maryland and the plaintiff sues the defendant in Maryland, then personal jurisdiction is not an issue because it's fair to sue defendants where they live.

So, what if the plaintiff in our opening hypothetical sued Hotel Ooh La La in Maryland? That's convenient for the plaintiff, who might live in Maryland, but the hotel is in Las Vegas, Nevada. Is it fair to force Hotel Ooh La La to schlep across the country to defend itself against the plaintiff's slip-and-fall in Vegas? Maybe the plaintiff is eighty-five years old and has poor eyesight and wasn't wearing her glasses that day. There's a really good argument that she should lose her lawsuit because the slip-and-fall was due to her own negligence—not the hotel's. Is it fair to force Hotel Ooh La La to spend the money to hire Maryland lawyers to try and get rid of the plaintiff's case in Maryland? All the witnesses to the event—and any videotape or hotel records—are in Vegas after all. Personal jurisdiction is a means of resolving whether it is fair to bring Hotel Ooh La La to Maryland.

How Hotel Ooh La La resolves this conundrum can have real consequences. If Hotel Ooh La La does absolutely nothing about the lawsuit believing that it's totally unfair to force it to go to Maryland to defend itself, then the Maryland court could issue what's known as a "default judgment." A default judgment would hand the plaintiff everything it asked for in the lawsuit because the defendant didn't bother to show up in the first instance. Hotel Ooh La La is in a pickle. It's a hard decision, and one that might benefit from hiring a lawyer, who will have to read prior decisions involving similar scenarios and do the "me too!" and "not it!" comparisons to prior cases to predict the hotel's chances in this case.

The law around personal jurisdiction spans many years and has many permutations. It all began with *Pennoyer*. In 1848, a young man named Marcus Neff left his home state of Iowa and headed west for Oregon. The same year, the U.S. Congress passed a statute establishing what was known officially as the Territory of Oregon, which included the current states of Oregon, Idaho, Washington, and parts of Montana and Wyoming.

The Territory of Oregon was in demand because the U.S. government had passed laws allowing people to acquire ownership of tracts of land west of the Mississippi River for free. They just had to go there and claim it. The goal of the laws was to encourage individual farmers to operate their own farms without using slave labor. Although the laws varied, most adults who hadn't taken up arms against the federal government could apply. Some laws allowed women, immigrants who had applied for citizenship, dispossessed Native Americans, and black Americans to apply too. The land freebie was attractive to many people.

Neff headed to Oregon to take advantage of this fantastic opportunity to obtain free land from the U.S. government. Under the law that applied to Oregon, claimants had to reside and cultivate the land for four years to obtain legal title to a plot. Neff fully completed his application, but fourteen years after his arrival in Oregon, he still hadn't received official title to the land from the U.S. government. The government gave title by mailing recipients a piece of paper known as a "land patent." Neff's hadn't come.

In 1862, he hired a lawyer, John H. Mitchell, and paid him $6.50 to submit a letter and an additional affidavit to the U.S. government to help him get his land patent. The affidavit stated that Neff had made improvements on the land as the law required. Within a year, Neff received notice from the government that he had met the criteria for a land patent, but the patent itself still hadn't arrived.

While Neff was waiting for his patent, he moved to California. In 1865, Mitchell sued Neff in Oregon state court, claiming that Neff owed him an additional $253.14 for legal services. Neff didn't respond to the lawsuit. Under Oregon law, if the defendant couldn't be found within the state, the plaintiff could give notice of the lawsuit simply by publishing information about it in a newspaper. Mitchell ran a notice for six weeks in the *Pacific Christian Advocate*, a weekly paper published by the Methodist Episcopal Church that focused on religious news. Not surprisingly, Neff didn't respond to the lawsuit. He didn't even know about it. The judge issued a default judgment against Neff and in favor of Mitchell for $253.14.

If you win a judgment in court directing another party to pay you money, there are several ways to actually get paid. The easiest way is if the other party writes you a check. If the other party refuses, then you can go back and get the government to force the sale of the defendant's property so you can get paid. (This is what happens when a bank forecloses on a mortgage, for example.)

Neff's land patent giving him title to the land in Oregon was sent from Washington, D.C., on March 22, 1866. But as Neff was in California then, he didn't know about the arrival of the land patent from Washington, D.C., any more than he knew about Mitchell's lawsuit. Mitchell knew that the patent would eventually come. He had done the work for Neff, after all.

Mitchell didn't act to get payment on his judgment immediately, however. Instead, he waited until August of 1866, after the land patent presumably arrived in Oregon. He went to the sheriff to force an auction of Neff's property—that is, the land that was granted to Neff by the federal government. He figured that the proceeds of the sale could be used to pay Mitchell's legal bill.

Guess who bought the land at the sheriff's auction? Mitchell himself, for $341.60. Scoundrel! Three days later, Mitchell sold the property to Sylvester Pennoyer, who took over the title that the sheriff issued to Mitchell following the auction. So now there were two titles to the same land—the one issued by the U.S. government, and the one issued by the sheriff following the auction that occurred to enforce the judgment in Mitchell's lawsuit. As I'll explain later, here's one place that *Pennoyer v. Neff* gets broken down into two parts: title number one to the property and title number two to the property. Which title to the property is the better one?

(It turns out that Mitchell was operating under an alias. His real name was John Hipple, a teacher from Pennsylvania who took up law after being forced to marry a fifteen-year-old student with whom he had sexual relations. In 1860, he went west with four thousand dollars in stolen client money and another girlfriend, whom he later abandoned in California. He moved to Portland, Oregon, changed his name to Mitchell, and remarried without divorcing his first young wife. Later in life, Mitchell was elected to the U.S. Senate. He was re-elected in 1885—after a public scandal involving love letters he'd written to the younger sister of his second wife during a five-year love affair. In 1905, while still serving in the Senate, Mitchell was convicted of land fraud, sentenced to six months in jail, and banned from holding public office. While his appeal was pending, he died from complications following a tooth extraction. The U.S. Senate adjourned on the day of his death without recognizing Mitchell, but later passed a resolution agreeing to pay his funeral expenses.)

After getting the sheriff-issued title to the Oregon property from Mitchell, Pennoyer merrily tended the land for eight years. But in 1874, Neff reappeared. Finding Pennoyer on the land, he sued Pennoyer that year, seeking to evict him. Neff won, and Pennoyer was thrown off the land he thought he owned. (By this time, Neff was well-off, with a wife and child, property, livestock, and even servants in San Joaquin, California.)

The matter made it all the way to the U.S. Supreme Court which ruled for Neff, explaining:

> A personal judgment is without any validity if it be rendered by a State court in an action upon a money demand against a nonresident of the State who was served by a publication of summons, but upon whom no personal service of process within the State was made, and who did not appear; and no title to property passes by a sale under an execution issued upon such a judgment.

Huh? If that's your reaction, you probably are in good company with the thousands of law students who read this case before you. This legal jargon seems unintelligible. How does one begin to make sense of *Pennoyer v. Neff*? The answer lies with Step 1: Break it down.

Applying Step 1

First, let's break down the facts. *Pennoyer v. Neff* is not about one lawsuit. It's about two lawsuits. The first one, if you recall, was between Mitchell and Neff. Mitchell sued Neff for the non-payment of legal fees. We can call that:

SUIT 1: *Mitchell v. Neff*

The second lawsuit came later, and it was between Neff and Pennoyer. Neff sued Pennoyer to kick him off the land. We can call that:

SUIT 2: *Pennoyer v. Neff*

Already, we have broken the case down into two parts—and we did it using only the facts, or what I call the "once upon a time" part of the case. Even in law school, the facts of most cases can be described as a story that begins with the familiar words, "Once upon a time . . ." At the end of the day, all cases are about a dispute between parties. Somebody was really mad at someone else. Why is everyone so angry with each other? This is one way to break down something really complex into something that makes common sense.

If we look a little deeper, we can break the case down even more. Why were the parties mad at each other in the second suit—the one that reached the U.S. Supreme Court? Well, Pennoyer thought he had good title to the Oregon land, and Neff thought he had good title to the land. Whose title was the better title? If Neff's was better, then Neff wins. If Pennoyer's was better, then Pennoyer wins. But whether Pennoyer's title was better depends on whether Mitchell had good title when he sold it to Pennoyer in the first place—which gets us back to SUIT 1, *Mitchell v. Neff.*

Now back to our emerging framework under Step 1:

SUIT 1: *Mitchell v. Neff.*
  Mitchell gets title through the sheriff's auction of the
    property, which he sells to Pennoyer.
SUIT 2: *Pennoyer v. Neff.*
  Neff gets title from the U.S. government.

So, the question is, which title is the better one? To answer this, we need to probe a bit deeper, and ask about the basis for each party's claim to the land. Neff got his from the U.S. government pursuant to a federal statute. That's probably a pretty good claim. Pennoyer got his from Mitchell who got his from the sheriff. The sheriff got the authority to sell the property to execute the judgment in SUIT 1, *Mitchell v. Neff*, in favor of Mitchell.

Was everything done properly in that lawsuit? Because if there was a problem with the judge issuing a judgment in favor of Mitchell for unpaid legal fees in the first place, then the sheriff had no legal right to sell the property, so the title issued by the sheriff to Mitchell was no good. And that's exactly what the U.S. Supreme Court held.

Recall the mystifying language quoted previously. The Supreme Court held that the judgment in SUIT 1 was issued "against a nonresident of the State who was served by a publication of summons, but upon whom no personal service of process within the State was made, and who did not appear." In other words, Mitchell was required to literally hand Neff a copy of the complaint initiating the lawsuit while Neff was on Oregon soil. This didn't happen, so the first judgment was invalid—as was Pennoyer's title to the property, which he got from Mitchell who got it from the sheriff after the auction to execute the judgment in SUIT 1.

Back again to our framework:

SUIT 1: *Mitchell v. Neff.*
> Mitchell gets title through the sheriff's auction of the property, which he sells to Pennoyer.
> **Title isn't good because there was no personal jurisdiction over the suit filed by Mitchell so he had no legal right to the property.**

SUIT 2: *Pennoyer v. Neff*
> Neff gets title from the U.S. government.
> **Title is good because it's from the U.S. government.**

The legal rule established in *Pennoyer v. Neff* is no longer the law governing personal jurisdiction—as I mentioned before, the Supreme Court has moved around a bit and the law has evolved substantially. But hopefully you can see how breaking the case down into its components helps get to the heart of the case—the issues that really mattered for purposes of deciding who should win. Those issues are: the quality of Pennoyer's title, which depends on the quality of the judgment in SUIT 1, on the one hand; and the quality of Neff's title on the other.

When students first read *Pennoyer v. Neff*, it comes across as one big glom. The issues and sub-issues are glommed all together under the heading "personal jurisdiction," and it's virtually impossible to make sense of the case on first blush. After completing the first semester of law school, and for the rest of most law students' lives, they never approach a complex problem the same way again. "Anti-glomming" becomes the new normal—and though it's a skill that people learn in law school, it can be used in everyday life too.

Employment Law Basics

Before we apply Step 1 to work life decisions, let's talk a bit about some of the rules that might come into play there. Employment law is its very own discipline. There are state and federal laws protecting employees from discrimination based on race, religion, sex, or sexual orientation; wage and hour laws protecting employees from unfair employer practices; and laws governing employees' privacy (including electronic privacy), drug testing, and work-related speech. In addition, each state has laws governing workers' compensation in the event of on-the-job injuries, and laws governing health care and other benefits, such as unemployment and disability insurance. There are federal laws governing the employment of non-citizens, protections for whistleblowers to complain about employers' unlawful practices, as well as safety and health laws for employees. Perhaps most pertinent to everyday life, each state has its own set of laws governing the creation of contracts, including employment contracts.

What should be in your own employment contract is a question that our legal framework might help you with. It can also help you determine whether it's okay and advisable to leave a particular job or whether you can be fired from one. For some jobs, there are laws and sometimes contract terms that identify limitations on what kinds of work you can do after you leave a particular position, and what information you must keep confidential.

As we will discuss in a later chapter, there are times in the employment context when you might decide that you need a lawyer because the laws and the intersecting factual issues can be complex. But for now, Step 1 in the framework can help break down the various questions that arise in deciding whether to accept or leave a job, and how to handle thorny issues that come up in the workplace. Just remember: Don't glom.

Taking a Job

Imagine this scenario: You just completed a bachelor's degree in web development with coursework under your belt in areas like computer programming and graphic design. You want a job building websites. Every business needs a website, so you figure you'll never be out of work. Eventually, you aspire to working almost entirely from home during hours you mostly set for yourself. For now, you need some solid experience with a reputable company. You understand you will start in a junior role and will have to work your way up. You apply to several employers, land an interview, and get an offer on the spot. What do you do now?

To begin with, remember the basic rule of human physiology: Don't make a decision reactively. Take your time. Breathe, thank the hiring manager for the offer, and say you will circle back soon. Just like the fight-or-flight response to stress, excitement can have strong physiological effects on the body, such as shaking, sweaty palms, a trembling voice, and redness in the face or neck. Your body releases chemicals that can reduce your motor, sensory, and visual functions, including language and memory. The endocrine system stimulates the production of the hormone adrenaline, which increases the flow of oxygen and glucose, dilates your pupils to enhance eyesight, and—as with a fear response—suppresses less urgent systems like digestion. It also makes people more ready, and likely, to act impulsively when emotions are running high. Retailers (and scam artists) know this—which is why it's easier to make a sale when a consumer is excited. As excited as you may be about a job offer, hold your proverbial horses. It can take twenty minutes for the body to move out of a state of arousal and return to homeostasis, or stability.

Once your body's excitement hormones have subsided, pull out Step 1 of the framework and break the decision down into its various components. Start with the biggest-picture issues and begin to build things out further like we did with *Pennoyer v. Neff.* The threshold issues might be:

Salary and benefits
Opportunities to progress

It is important to keep this initial list short. Try to be as comprehensive as possible in your categories. You might need to edit them as you go along. Salary and benefits could encompass several things, from base salary to a salary cap, bonus potential, annual leave, pension or other savings programs, and health care, to working remotely or having a company-issued laptop. By the same token, opportunities to progress could include initial work responsibilities, whom you will report to, and job location (maybe you begin in a satellite office and work toward a transfer to the home office, for example).

Once you have the primary categories down, you can identify the sub-issues, as we did with *Pennoyer v. Neff.* It might look something like this:

SALARY AND BENEFITS

Pay

Pay cap

Bonus

Overtime

Job security

Health care

Pension

401(k)

Laptop

Company car or mileage reimbursement

Life insurance

Disability insurance

Administrative assistance

Training allowance or support

Flexibility of hours

Remote work opportunities
Holidays and sick leave

OPPORTUNITIES TO PROGRESS
Initial responsibilities
Pathways for promotion
Management structure
Management opportunities
Training allowance or support

You might want to gather some additional data under one or more of these issues. According to the U.S. Bureau of Labor Statistics, for example, the median annual wage for a web developer in May 2019 was $73,760. (A median is a value in the middle of a range of numbers—the median of 1 and 10 is 5.) So, when you go back to the hiring official, you'll know now whether your offer is fair. If your offer is low, you now have in mind what number you believe would be fair to you, and what a number might be that's so low that you just cannot accept it under any circumstances. A fair number might be $73,000, and a walk-away number might be $65,000, for example.

From this list, ask yourself: "Which is *the most important* of the two initial categories?" Rank them. Then ask, "What are the most important issues that fall under each of those categories?" Rank those sub-issues too.

For example, a member of a young couple hoping to have children might factor flexible hours or remote working opportunities higher than a single person straight out of college. If the job applicant has other offers in hand, that person might add the other offer to this list to compare and contrast what aspects of which job look better—much like we did when we compared Pennoyer's title to the Oregon property with Neff's title. On second thought, some factors might fall off as unimportant at this stage. For the person who is married and wants kids soon, a revised list might look something like this:

SALARY AND BENEFITS
Pay
Job security
Health care
~~Pay cap~~
~~Bonus~~
Flexibility of hours
Remote work opportunities
Holidays and sick leave
Overtime
Life insurance
Disability insurance
Pension or 401(k)
Administrative assistance
Training allowance or support
~~Laptop~~
~~Company car or mileage reimbursement~~

OPPORTUNITIES TO PROGRESS
Initial responsibilities
Management structure

Training allowance or support

Pathways for promotion

~~Management opportunities~~

As you can see from this hypothetical, the person thinking of having a baby prioritized salary and benefits over opportunities to progress. Under salary and benefits, that person prioritized things like flexibility of hours and remote working opportunities over having a company car, on the expectation that those things will become increasingly important if a child is involved. Under opportunities to progress, the subject of management structure—which might capture the management style of the individual the person will be working for, and whether that boss supports a balance between work and family—is ranked more highly than promotion opportunities. (I know this all might sound gendered, but as a working mother of four, I can tell you these are realistic—and often very difficult—choices for many women.)

Once you've done this ranking, sleep on things for a while. Researchers believe that the brain may habitually review events of the day while sleeping. I discovered this for myself when I was in law school. Never an all-nighter kind of person, I knew that I'd turn into a pumpkin at midnight regardless of how well I knew the material for an exam the next day. So, I inevitably went to bed early enough so I could sleep at least seven hours. What I discovered was this: If I read over my notes passively before going to sleep and simply asked my brain to review them throughout the night, when I woke up, I could recite the information pretty much cold. It turns out that our brains do actively process memories during sleep, so if you want your brain to continue ruminating over a decision you are facing, it might be worth passively "telling" it to do so before you drift off. In the morning, you might be surprised by the clarity that emerged overnight.

The next day, underline those factors that you might consider what I call "the heart" of the decision for you. These might come straight from your gut. The heart of the decision is what you will go back to if you feel confused, distracted, or overwhelmed at any point in the process. It's your lighthouse. It's how you will separate the wheat from the chaff and keep your eye on the main prize. It also helps you feel okay about the decision if things don't work out like you'd hoped. For a working parent with primary childcare responsibilities, for example, the heart of my hypothetical decision might include flexibility of hours and remote working opportunities for decent pay.

Now on to a few final lawyerly tips on contract negotiation. Not every employer memorializes the terms of employment in a retention letter or contract, but it's almost always a good idea to do so, because it settles unsettled terms before they come up for debate. When reviewing your own contract, check that it includes things like:

- Both the employer and employee's full legal names
- The date the employment begins
- The pay rate and frequency of payment
- Job title
- Sick leave
- Holidays
- The conditions under which the contract can be terminated by either or both parties

- A job description—that is, your work responsibilities in exchange for your wages

It's also a good idea to include any confidentiality agreements, details on the company's technology privacy policies, and any restrictions on your employment after you terminate the contract.

Keep in mind too that a contract is only a piece of paper. It's important that you feel good about the values and trustworthiness of your employer, because if the contract is breached, the only remedy is to file a lawsuit in court for breach of contract—much like Mitchell did in the first lawsuit in *Pennoyer v. Neff*. This can be prohibitively expensive, time-consuming, and stressful. Oftentimes, having a clear employment contract can forestall litigation because the key provisions are agreed-upon in advance. There's nothing of importance left for a judge to decide.

Managing a Job

Now let's apply the framework thus far to a new hypothetical—a difficult problem at work. Suppose that you are assigned to a client to develop a website and a more junior person in the firm is assigned to assist. The junior person is younger and less experienced but prized by the firm because of a perceived "fire in the belly"—or aggressive drive to succeed. The manager doesn't want to tamp that down, so the company is very careful not to push back on the junior person's sometimes clunky efforts to obtain more responsibility.

The first step in the assignment is to meet with the client

and get a sense of what the client wants for the website. The two of you attend the initial meeting, and all goes well. You run the meeting and get the information you need. Afterwards, you call the junior associate and talk through your initial thoughts for the website. You decide that you need market research on other existing websites in the same industry as the client. You ask the junior associate to take on that project, set a deadline, and arrange for a follow-up meeting with the client in two weeks' time. You get started on a formal proposal for the site.

A week goes by, and the junior associate hasn't given you any information about competing sites. When you follow up, you find out that the associate has already spoken with your manager about the client meeting—without looping you in. The manager is excited about the junior associate's enthusiasm and ignores the fact that the associate sidelined you. The manager also mentions the initial research the associate did. You weren't copied on it, so that comes as a surprise. You ask that it be forwarded to you. The manager sends you the email with the associate's work. You then email the associate requesting some follow-up research. The associate responds, "You go ahead and do whatever research you need, and I will add it to my memo later." Translation? The junior member is not going to treat you as a senior member of the team, is lobbing the assignment back to you, and may even be actively working to ice you out. Worse, the manager is not going to back you, because the higher-ups feel that the junior associate is the future of the firm. What do you do?

Remember the threshold rule is to avoid reacting. You might be angry, and rightfully so. Your instinct is to tell off the associate, complain to the manager, or both. At a minimum, you draft an email with very strong language for both of them. Your finger lingers over the send button, but then you remember to wait at least thirty minutes. The hormones are surging because your brain thinks you are in some sort of danger. The situation is annoying, but dangerous it is not. Take a few breaths and wait awhile.

Once your heartbeat has returned to normal and your palms are dry again, the next objective is to break the problem down. What are the major issues here? They might be as follows:

Job security
Respectful working environment

Breaking the issue down this way could bring some immediate clarity. If the junior associate is able to ultimately make you redundant, it's conceivable that you will lose your job to that person if nothing changes, so job security is important to identify. The second major category is important to your overall quality of life, but it may be less urgent in the long run. The most critical thing is to have a job. The secondary priority is to have a job that works for you—where you feel valued and are treated accordingly.

You prioritize the two major categories and then identify the sub-issues under each. Here's what the next formulation might look like:

JOB SECURITY
Family's financial needs
Competitiveness of the job in terms of salary and benefits

Other potential job opportunities
Company culture of loyalty to employees (i.e., is there any
    serious chance of being fired because of politics?)

RESPECTFUL WORKING ENVIRONMENT
Job satisfaction as a priority in your life
Your relationship with management
Your relationship with the junior associate
Your tolerance for conflict
Opportunities for improving the situation

Framed this way, it might become evident that financial
security is the most important issue, at least for now. Accordingly, you might want to focus on opportunities for improvement
within the firm. At the same time, perhaps you begin to explore
other potential job opportunities outside the firm as "insurance"
if things don't come around. So, you need to decide what to do
about the associate's behavior in an effort to improve. You decide
to look at opportunities for improvement with an eye towards
preserving the job as your top priority.

The next step, then, might be to break down the "opportunities for improvement" category even further:

OPPORTUNITIES FOR IMPROVEMENT
Talk to the associate about the behavior
Talk to management about the behavior
Ignore the behavior and focus on other things in your life
Get the advice of friends or trusted advisors first

Once you have this list, you might decide to sleep on things and tell your brain to think about the options overnight. The decision might be clearer in the morning.

Although the problem isn't yet solved, applying Step 1 of our legal framework to this hypothetical workplace conflict achieved some of what law professors work toward in class. It avoided the dreaded glom—where the issues are all piled on top of each other, leaving students feeling overwhelmed and even defeated, and making access to a good decision seem impossible. It identified the heart of the matter moving forward—job retention—as well as a list of potential steps toward resolution, in order of priority.

Imagine, then, that you decide to approach the junior associate, who gets defensive. When you articulate your concerns further, explaining that this kind of behavior is counterproductive for the client, the associate goes on the offensive. So much for working things out that way. You might then decide to talk to management or just live with things for now. In the interim, you could investigate other job opportunities. Even if you ultimately stay with the same employer, knowing the relative value of that position in terms of other options—particularly given that the heart of the matter for you is job security—could be helpful. If you ultimately wind up tolerating the junior associate's obnoxiousness, you have better information for justifying that choice now.

As we build out the framework through the rest of the book, I invite you to go back to these initial hypotheticals and add the next steps to the decision-making analysis. This is precisely how

I teach law students how to think like lawyers. We learn a foundational skill, apply it to a hypothetical problem, then add the next brick in the wall to that skill. When students ask me for sample exam problems at the end of the semester, I point them to the early hypotheticals and encourage revisiting them with the newer skill in hand. With more steps in the legal method under their belts, those earlier problems can be addressed more richly, thoroughly, and productively the second time around. The same can be said for readers of this book.

Leaving a Job

Imagine lastly that you are faced with having to decide whether to leave your job. Maybe the problems with the junior associate got to be too much for you. Maybe a headhunter called you out of the blue with a great opportunity, but it's in Pittsburgh and you live in Los Angeles. Maybe you just had your third child and cannot handle the hours with three small kids at home but want to stay in the workforce.

Hopefully, you know the drill by now. The first thing to keep in mind is the importance of not making any big decisions when stress or excitement hormones are raging. Maybe you got the Pittsburgh job, and it's double the salary. In the moment, you are thrilled and feel an urge to accept. Or maybe you find out from the client that the junior associate submitted a proposal behind your back—the client just figured you had already signed off. Your blood pressure surges as you shake your head in disbelief. Don't react. Give your body time to return to its more normal hormonal state.

Next, break the problem down. Start by listing two or three categories of issues, then move on to sub-issues. Sleep on it with intention and prioritize the categories and sub-categories the next day. Circle the heart of the matter, and cross off items that you don't feel strongly about one way or another. Then, once you are through this book, apply Steps 2 through 5 to the results.

As you go along applying the framework, I also encourage you to sit with the experience a bit after each step. How do you feel compared to times in the past when you had to make big decisions but didn't really have a defined process for doing so? Does this feel different? If so, does it feel better? Or maybe it's too tedious for you. If the latter, keep in mind that—as we discussed earlier in the book—not every decision needs a step-by-step decision tree to turn out well. Some choices are best made in reliance on gut instincts or past experiences. This book just provides another tool in your life toolbox. Kind of like hiring a lawyer, eh?

STEP 1 CHECKLIST: BREAK IT DOWN

✓ First, consider the decision on the table (feel free to "glom" here).

✓ Next, break the decision down into components—begin with at least two.

✓ Break each component of your initial list into sub-issues—begin with at least two for each, if you can.

✓ Prioritize your list into most important component to least important.

✓ Circle the "heart" ♥ of the decision.

2

Thinking Like a Lawyer
in Family Life Decisions

Divorce is a game played by lawyers.
—CARY GRANT

Throughout any individual's life cycle, an untold number of family-oriented decisions arise: Should I marry? Should I have a child? If so, when? If the family can afford it, should one parent stay home with the kids? If not, should the children go into daycare, or should the family hire a caregiver? If we hire someone, should that someone live in our house to care for the kids? And how do we find the right person? What about religion—one parent is Jewish and the other Christian. How should the kids be raised?

Families make choices nearly every day, from where to go for dinner to choosing a vacation spot. With multiple people involved, figuring out how to foster communication and achieve consensus can be tough, if not impossible, at times. This chapter applies basic lawyering skills to family decision-making, with particular emphasis on Step 2 of the framework: Identify your values and your aim.

Studies show that a traditional "life cycle" for individuals and families often begins with single people in their twenties. They marry or decide to live with another person. The couple has children. The children leave the nest. The couple might divorce at some point, or if they stay together, the death of an individual's spouse winds up leaving the person back at the beginning of the cycle, albeit many years older.

But of course, things are much more complicated in real life. Some people never marry, never have children, or have children but raise them as a single parent. In a marriage scenario, if the couple divorces while the children are at home, the family may become two households. One or both individuals might remarry, perhaps to an individual who also has kids, creating "blended" households. For many people, single parenting is the norm at that juncture—the second step in the traditional life cycle isn't part of their lives. Some state laws even recognize three-person parenting, with all three adults sharing legal custody of a child. In fact, a Pew Research report from 2014 found that fewer than half of American kids live in a family that resembles the traditional life cycle with two married parents in their first marriage. Families come in many shapes and sizes.

Education presents another stream of choices. Should the kids go to private school (if that's even affordable)? Or imagine that grandma is paying the child's tuition. How much influence should she be allowed to have in the child's upbringing? What kinds of recreational activities should the kids be involved in—and how much should parents push kids if they resist? Then, of course, there's the monster of social media, which is very challenging for children and parents alike. When should a child be allowed to have a phone or a TikTok account? And how should parents manage screen time and website access for young kids?

Deciding how to discipline kids raises a whole host of tricky parenting issues, too, which differ depending on a child's age and personality. Should a teen be allowed to sleep over at a friend's house when you don't know the parents? What about kids' demands to dye their hair purple or pierce their noses? And should you emphasize to your child that it's important to get good grades, and maybe even help with homework to the point of jumping in and actually doing some of it?

Perhaps most importantly, what if parents disagree on how to address any of these questions?

Some of these decisions involve bargaining and trade-offs, to be sure, but lawyering skills can come into play in at least two ways. First, they can help you prepare to make these choices by identifying things like the family's core values with some specificity and buy-in from the individuals involved. Second, the framework outlined in this book offers a methodical process for moving through family decision-making. At a minimum, it can help you feel some measure of control and clarity in sometimes overwhelming life moments.

Many families do not include children, of course—and they face lots of big decisions as well. You know it's time to buy a car or a house—but which one? Or where? And when is the right time to make such a huge purchase? How to make and implement a family budget—particularly if members of the family have different risk tolerances and spending behaviors? And then there are the mundane day-to-day tasks like keeping the home clean, going grocery shopping, cooking dinner, taking out the trash, replacing a lightbulb, and walking the dog. Who does what and how to decide?

As with other categories of decision-making, there's a lot of research and opinions out there about how families make decisions. Socio-economic status, education, income, and family size all affect how family decision-making processes unfold. Factors like the relative competence and expertise of one partner over the other, the importance of a decision to one person in the family as compared to others, whether one person tends to play a dominant role in decision-making already, and any competing problems that are pressing on the family can all affect how decisions unfold in family life.

Let's return to the five-part B-I-C-A-T framework for legal decision-making that we discussed in the introduction to this book:

1. **Break** the problem down.
2. **Identify** your values and your aim.
3. **Collect** lots of knowledge.
4. **Argue** both sides of each point.
5. **Tolerate** the fact that people will disagree with your choice—and that you might feel conflicted.

In this chapter, we will focus on **Step 2: Identify your values and your aim.**

In the first chapter, we covered the first step in the

framework—breaking things down into smaller problems. As a recap, let's first apply that step to a family life decision.

Applying B-I-C-A-T Step 1

Imagine that a couple must decide whether to move out of an apartment and purchase a house, or whether it would be better to wait. The landlord is raising the rent and requiring a two-year lease, so the time is ripe for moving. Under Step 1, the couple would break down the decision into several sub-issues, such as:

- **Finances.** This includes a rundown of monthly income, fixed expenses, other long-term financial goals, and the amount of savings in the bank that's available for a down payment.
- **Housing Market.** Whether to buy a house right away—or whether to wait two more years until the new lease expires—would depend on the neighborhood that the couple wants to buy in and the state of the market that time of year. If the inventory of houses is flush, a home could be available at a bargain price now but would be harder to resell in the short-term. If there are relatively few houses for sale, the couple might have to pay a premium for the house, but it could hold its value better as an investment because of its prized location.
- **Lifestyle.** Often, a young couple is not yet at a peak earning phase of life. The cost of purchasing a first home can be daunting, and certainly greater than the

cost of renting. As a result, first homes are often in a less desirable location than a one-bedroom apartment in the heart of a city, for example. Or maybe the couple is ready to have kids, so being in an excellent school district is relatively more important.

Any substantial family decision can be broken down into its components. Where to send a child to school triggers budget considerations, location, as well as a child's particular educational needs. How to manage a teenager's screen time, might entail sub-issues like the cost of a phone or laptop, school schedules and extra-curricular obligations, and how important screen time is to the child. If it's very important and the child tends to be difficult to manage, then a parent might want to use screen time as a means of motivating positive behavior. If the child uses screens to learn dance moves during the COVID-19 pandemic, then the physical exercise might be worth the extra time gazing at a phone. This process of breaking down a problem into smaller bytes is precisely what law professors impress on students facing a question of law or a strategic dilemma for a client.

When students come to law school, they usually assume at least two things. First, they assume that they will be learning a bunch of rules, and that rules are black and white. Stop at a red light, accelerate at a green light. Wear a seatbelt while driving. Turn off all electronic devices during airplane take-off and landing. All of these rules are grounded in laws. State and local laws identify traffic rules. The Congress and its statutory bureaucratic creations, known as the Department of Transportation and the Federal Aviation Administration, issue laws governing airline safety, and so on.

Students learn quickly that this is *rarely* correct. Law—like life—is not black and white, but many shades of gray. Accepting the fact that the answers are not clear or readily accessible is perhaps the greatest hurdle of a first-year law student. Once a student gives up on trying to find "the" answer, the student is on the path to thinking like a lawyer. We will learn more about hashing out the various shades of gray in later chapters. But for now, hold on tightly to the notion that black-and-white thinking is not how lawyers work—it's cancerous to their ability to practice well. This means that letting go of the immediate need to find a quick-and-dirty answer—and to be 100% "right" about it by all accounts—is crucial to making everyday decisions in ways that simulate the skills learned in elite law schools.

The second thing that new law students often assume is that the law cares a lot about their personal opinions on issues of fairness and justice. This assumption, once again, is flawed. Unless you wind up becoming a judge—and even then, only if you become a judge on one of the highest courts in the land, like the U.S. Supreme Court—your opinion on issues of fairness and justice is hardly pivotal in a courtroom. Some law students become lawmakers or regulators, and in those capacities, their personal views on justice might bear on how they craft legislation and rules. But for most lawyers, just doing what you believe to be "right" is not how the job works.

That is not to say, however, that values don't matter in the practice of law. They do. It's just that they don't matter in the way that non-lawyers think about values. In the framework for decision-making outlined in this book, values come into play at numerous points—which is why it's important to identify what they are from the outset.

Here's another classroom example to help illustrate the difference between just doing what you think is right on the one hand and bringing personal values to bear in the way lawyers do legal analysis on the other.

A Law School Lesson: *Scott v. Harris*

How Do Values Come into Play in Legal Arguments by Lawyers and Decisions by Judges?

In one of my courses, we discuss a Supreme Court case called *Scott v. Harris.* The case involves a high-speed car chase that occurred in Georgia in 2001. The driver, Victor Harris, an African American man, was going 73 miles per hour in a 55-mile-per-hour speed limit zone. A sheriff's deputy activated his blue flashing lights, but rather than pull over, the driver accelerated to speeds exceeding 85 miles per hour. The officer radioed his dispatch to report that he was pursuing a fleeing vehicle. Another sheriff's deputy, Timothy Scott, heard the call and joined the pursuit. At one point, Harris pulled into a parking lot of a shopping center to face a cluster of police vehicles. After making a sharp turn and colliding with Deputy Scott's car, Harris sped off again on the two-lane highway, with Scott taking over in the pursuit.

Approximately six minutes and ten miles after the chase began, Scott radioed his supervisor for permission to end the episode through use of a "Precise Intervention Technique" or "PIT" maneuver, which involved hitting Harris's rear bumper to cause the car to spin and ultimately stop. Scott executed the maneuver, which caused Harris to lose control of his car, careen down an embankment, overturn, and crash. The episode left the nineteen-year-old Harris a quadriplegic. He sued the police officer for money damages.

Keep in mind that every lawsuit requires first and foremost a legal cause of action. What that means is that some source of law—a statute passed by a legislature or the text of the U.S. Constitution, for example—must create a legal limit that the other side allegedly crossed, and it must also provide for some sort of relief to the victim if the victim can prove that the line was actually crossed. Here, Harris's cause of action dwelt in the Fourth Amendment to the U.S. Constitution, which bans the government from conducting unreasonable searches and seizures. The most obvious historical example of an unreasonable search might be a group of British soldiers randomly ransacking an American colonist's home in 1775 to find out if there is hidden evidence—say, a pamphlet or letter—suggesting that the head of the household is part of a rebellion against the Crown.

The idea behind the Fourth Amendment's ban on unreasonable searches and seizures is that the government must have evidence in hand that gives rise to what's called "probable cause"—and usually a warrant from a judge—before it can go barging into someone's private domain to fish around for information that can be held against the occupants. Harris's argument was that, by performing the PIT maneuver to stop Harris from driving really fast, Scott performed an unreasonable search and seizure of Harris himself because the force of Scott's car was unconstitutionally excessive. His legal claim was a valid one. But Harris lost his case in the Supreme Court by an 8 to 1 vote.

Though there are more nuances to the legalities of Harris's claim, the case boiled down to whether Harris posed a threat to pedestrians or motorists by driving so fast. If he did, then Scott's use of the PIT maneuver was reasonable and there were no grounds to find him liable for violating the Fourth Amendment. If Harris was not endangering others, then Scott was potentially on the hook to pay Harris for his injuries as a matter of the U.S. Constitution itself.

But here's the catch that made the case noteworthy in comparison to older Fourth Amendment cases: two videotapes were taken from squad cars during the high-speed chase. The videos were black-and-white and grainy, but clearly showed Harris speeding. In his majority opinion, Justice Antonin Scalia described the scene this way:

> There we see respondent's vehicle racing down narrow, two-lane roads in the dead of night at speeds that are shockingly fast. We see it swerve around more than a dozen other cars, cross the double-yellow line, and force cars traveling in both directions to their respective shoulders to avoid being hit. We see it run multiple red lights and travel for considerable periods of time in the occasional center left-turn-only lane, chased by numerous police cars forced to engage in the same hazardous maneuvers just to keep up. Far from being the cautious and controlled driver the lower court depicts, what we see on the video more closely resembles a Hollywood-style car chase of the

most frightening sort, placing police officers and innocent bystanders alike at great risk of serious injury.

In the view of eight justices on the U.S. Supreme Court who agreed to toss out the case, the video was proof-positive that Scott acted reasonably because Harris was putting others in harm's way. Case closed.

Justice John Paul Stevens, alone, dissented. This was his take:

[Harris] was on a four-lane portion of Highway 34 when the officer clocked his speed at 73 miles per hour and initiated the chase. More significant . . . the sirens and flashing lights on the police cars following respondent gave the same warning that a speeding ambulance or fire engine would have provided. The 13 cars that respondent passed on his side of the road before entering the shopping center, and both of the cars that he passed on the right after leaving the center, no doubt had already pulled to the side of the road or were driving along the shoulder because they heard the police sirens or saw the flashing lights before respondent or the police cruisers approached.

[Harris] and his pursuers went through only two intersections with stop lights and in both cases all other vehicles in sight were stationary, presumably because they had been warned of the approaching speeders. . . . In any event, the risk of harm to the stationary vehicles was minimized by the sirens, and there is no reason to believe that respondent would have disobeyed the signals if he were not being pursued.

[P]assing a slower vehicle on a two-lane road always involves some degree of swerving and is not especially dangerous if there are no cars coming from the opposite direction. At no point during the chase did respondent pull into the opposite lane other than to pass a car in front of him; he did the latter no more than five times and, on most of those occasions, used his turn signal. On none of these occasions was there a car traveling in the opposite direction. In fact, at one point, when respondent found himself behind a car in his own lane and there were cars traveling in the other direction, he slowed and waited for the cars traveling in the other direction to pass before overtaking the car in front of him while using his turn signal to do so. This is hardly the stuff of Hollywood. To the contrary, the video does not reveal any incidents that could even be remotely characterized as "close calls."

Having watched the actual videos (the YouTube links are available in the notes to this book), law students inevitably tend to fall into one of two staunch camps: those who believe that the deputy sheriff was totally out of line and that Harris's paralysis warranted compensation, and those who believe that speeding is speeding and that Harris took the risk that he'd be injured by failing to pull over in the first place. These differing camps undoubtedly derive in part from students' individual life experiences. Almost every year, there is at least one student who has served in a law enforcement capacity and understands the stress, complexities, and strain that Scott was facing in those harried moments. There are also usually several students who have had bad encounters with police—often around race—and feel strongly that the Supreme Court thwarted justice by sending Harris away empty-handed to live his life in a wheelchair, without any compensation from the government for his fate at the hands of county law enforcement.

It may come as a surprise to learn that the court's majority in *Scott v. Harris* included not only the notoriously conservative Justice Scalia—along with fellow conservatives Samuel Alito, John Roberts, and Clarence Thomas—but also Justices Ruth Bader Ginsberg and Stephen Breyer, who have more liberal reputations. (Also in the majority were Justices Anthony Kennedy and David Souter.) It's fair to say, then, that the outcome of the case did not obviously turn on personal views of fairness and justice. If it did, we might have expected Justice Ginsberg to have joined Justice Stevens in dissent, for example, on the assumption that providing some monetary support for the permanently disabled youth was the right thing to do—particularly given that there were two sides to the story—at least based on the competing accounts of Justices Scalia and Stevens, who are Supreme Court Justices and thus presumably reasonable people, after all.

But that's not how lawyers make decisions. Remember the bedrock principle of thinking like a lawyer that was mentioned earlier: Hard decisions are rarely black and white. They almost always involve many shades of gray. In wading through the grayscale, lawyers rely on more than their own intuition and sense of fairness. (In fact, if they did only that, they might wind up committing malpractice.) Lawyers must start with the law—that is, the official rules governing conduct in society. The Fourth Amendment bans unreasonable searches and seizures. The question in

Scott v. Harris was not about the fair or compassionate thing to do for Mr. Harris or Mr. Scott (who, after all, was just doing his job; and if the case had gone forward, it was possible that he'd have to pay a huge amount of money out of his own pocket—not government coffers). The question was whether what Scott did under the circumstances was a reasonable thing for a police officer to do.

The concept of reasonableness thus confined the judges' ability to simply do what they saw fit as a matter of their own personal values or politics. In that way, judges are different from politicians. They cannot just create laws that they think society needs, or change laws that they think need changing, or award money to parties they happen to like, or order payment from parties they happen to dislike. They must operate within the rules. And in this case, the rules demanded that the Justices decide the case around reasonableness—not some intrinsic or personal view of how the dispute should resolve. Their discretion, in other words, was limited.

However—and this is where personal values inevitably creep into legal reasoning—"reasonableness" is a squishy concept. What's reasonable to you might be different from what's reasonable to me. We see this every day in our regular lives. For some people, showing up ten minutes late for a lunch date is reasonable, particularly in a city like Washington, D.C., or Los Angeles, where traffic can be crushing and unpredictable. For others, it is unreasonable and rude. If you live in one of those cities, maybe you should factor in that it's important to leave an extra ten minutes for bad traffic. Translated into a potential value system, then, one person might value flexibility and ease—and the ability to engage in personal relationships that are similarly forgiving when it comes to things like being a few minutes late—while for other people, timeliness is more highly valued, because it allows for order and certitude and shows extra respect for others. Values inevitably matter even when applying rules.

Now back to the framework, and Step 2: Identify your values and your aim.

Identifying Your Values

We all have a general notion of what "values" mean, but it's helpful to pin down a definition and put words to the concept. Daphna Oyserman, a professor of psychology at the University of Southern California, defines the term "values" as the "internalized cognitive structures that guide choices by evoking a sense of basic principles of right and wrong (e.g., moral values), as well as priorities (e.g., personal achievement vs. group good)." The notion of right and wrong strikes a very primal chord, but of course it's more complicated than those two poles. "Think of ethics, law, religion, politics, education, art, lifestyle, child rearing, and more," Oyserman explains. It's an amorphous concept, to be sure.

On both a personal and societal level, what is certain is that values can influence behavior. A value system can affect how one thinks about an issue (that is, the cognitive or logical response to it), and how one feels about it. Moreover, the effects of a value system on a decision can be explicit or implicit—we might not even realize how much our values are having an impact on how we view a particular choice. For example, we probably know people who reflexively go along with the official policy platform of one or the other major national political parties in the United States, regardless of its merits. They might highly value being part of a group—without even realizing that it's their value system's emphasis on belonging that's mostly driving things, not the pros and cons of the party's position on each issue at stake in a particular election.

Nonetheless, values can be hard to identify and articulate, in part because they are context-specific. A person might place great value on having a spotless home but feel perfectly comfortable camping out in the woods without running water for a few days. Values also vary by culture, age, education, personal and professional experiences, socio-economic status, race, and religion. What seems wrong, unnatural, or immoral to one group—like consuming cows, for example, which are sacred in the Hindu tradition—could be considered perfectly acceptable, natural, and moral to others.

An important insight—and one that lawyers habitually bear in mind—is that value systems are extremely important to society at large, as well. They operate to sustain the social order. What's "fair" is determined in part by our broadly shared value systems. In the United States, for example, we value social order in ways that other countries do not. Rules like stopping at stop signs operate to prevent vehicle-related injuries and overall chaos, which American culture values. In some countries, traffic laws are non-existent or ignored, and it's just a part of life to drive more defensively in those cultures. At fast-food restaurants in the United States, people patiently and habitually line up behind open cash registers before placing an order. In other countries, like China, queuing is replaced with something more like a free-for-all. In my experience visiting there, if someone comes up behind you and catches the service worker's attention before you do, it doesn't matter that you were there first. The intruder gets the priority.

One reason that Americans wait in line might be an adherence to a value system that includes fairness. "First come, first served" seems like a fair way to manage a crowd. Furthermore, individuals are more likely to accept and follow laws and rules if they believe those laws and rules are fair and fairly applied. As Professor Oyserman explains, "[v]alues are not simply individual traits, they are social agreements about what is right, good, to be cherished."

In the case of *Scott v. Harris*, one Justice might have personally placed a high value on ensuring, say, that Harris had the financial support he needed to live the rest of his life with a severe disability. But that had nothing to do with the reasonableness of the deputy sheriff's actions. For that question, only broader social values legitimately came into play. Lawyers and judges refer to such values as "policy" rationales.

For Justice Scalia, public safety was paramount. He explained that "Scott defends his actions by pointing to the paramount governmental interest in ensuring public safety." If officers had to worry constantly about being sued for doing their jobs, they might not take the risks that are sometimes inherently necessary to keep people safe in urgent situations. Moreover, Scalia reasoned that Harris "posed an actual and imminent threat to the lives of any pedestrians who might have been present, to other civilian motorists, and to the officers involved in the chase." Scalia went on to ask and answer a rhetorical question: "But wait, says respondent: Couldn't the innocent public equally have been protected, and the tragic accident entirely avoided, if the police had simply ceased their pursuit? We think the police need not have taken that chance and hoped for the best. Whereas Scott's action—ramming respondent off the road—was *certain* to eliminate the risk that respondent posed to the public, ceasing pursuit was not."

Moreover, Scalia reasoned, if Harris were allowed to proceed with his case, the value in public safety would be thwarted more generally. Scalia explained that a decision in Harris's favor would: "Lay down a rule requiring the police to allow fleeing suspects to get away whenever they drive *so recklessly* that they put other people's lives in danger. It is obvious the perverse incentives such a rule would create: Every fleeing motorist would know that escape is within his grasp, if only he accelerates to 90 miles per hour, crosses the double-yellow line a few times, and runs a few red lights."

Justice Stevens was less concerned about public safety, and more concerned about taking that kind of policy judgment out of the hands of judges. His approach valued judicial restraint over the values emphasized by Scalia—that is, the need to stave off reckless drivers to protect the public. For Justice Stevens, the facts were sufficiently vague that the case should have gone to a jury instead of being truncated by a bunch of unelected judges on the U.S. Supreme Court. Essentially, what the majority held was that the reasonableness of Scott's actions was so obvious and clear that there was no reason to allow the case to go to trial, because any jury that awarded damages to Harris would be defying logic and common sense. For Stevens, keeping judges from exercising too much discretion—and leaving big value-based decisions to legislators who have to answer to the public at the ballot box or to juries who are operating as the parties' own peers—was more important than the hypothetical impact on public safety that a decision for Harris would have created.

I hope this discussion illuminates a bit how lawyers employ values in decision-making, how their use of values is different from how most people use them in everyday life, and why it's important to identify the values involved before making a big decision utilizing the kinds of skills that lawyers use. If nothing else, naming the values that influence you can help you make a more informed decision in terms of the driving forces behind it. Let's now go back to the topic of making family life decisions, and how identifying your values can help with those decisions.

Family Law Basics

Most law schools offer a course in family law, which itself might sound like a contradiction in terms. Families are about interpersonal relationships, psychology, genetics, socio-economics, personal histories, and—not to put too fine a point on it—love. The word *law* is defined more coldly and clinically:

> The system of rules which a particular country or community recognizes as regulating the actions of its members and which it may enforce by the imposition of penalties.

Law is largely about rules and penalties. How do these apply to families?

The traditional family law curriculum in law school covers topics like marriage and divorce, custody and support of children, and the processes for resolving family disputes. Lawyers get involved before marriages occur for purposes of drafting prenuptial agreements, which are designed to avoid costly legal battles in the event of divorce. The agreements—or contracts—set forth the governing rules in the event of a divorce (sometimes they are drafted after the marriage). Lawyers may be invoked later, too, for purposes of divorce, child custody and support, and other related matters.

Keep in mind that marriage itself is a legal construct—in addition to a religious one in many traditions. By legal construct, I mean that the government establishes the marriage as a matter of law and recognizes the relationship with a marriage license. The state's legislative body decides on the criteria that people need to satisfy to secure a marriage license. It also decides on the standards for dissolving a legal marriage, as well as the rules that apply for dividing up property and determining the custody and care of any children.

To obtain a divorce, at least one person in the marriage usually has to file a lawsuit asking a court to nullify the legal construct of marriage that the state established with a marriage license. The way lawsuits are started is by filing a piece of paper known as a "complaint," which sets forth the facts according to the plaintiff as well as the law giving the plaintiff the right to the relief they request. Divorce proceedings are no different—a complaint is filed, asking the court to legally dissolve the marriage, explaining the facts of the situation, and citing the provisions of law governing divorce in that state. Lawyers often draft these documents, although not necessarily. People can seek a divorce without the help of lawyers, but if the couple is especially angry with each other or lots of money is involved, lawyers almost inevitably become involved.

Divorce cases boil down to two issues: stuff and children. By stuff, I am referring to the division of money in the bank accounts, securities and other equity holdings, and literally the contents involving a home—from glassware and plates to cars and televisions. Stuff also includes the concept of alimony, which is different from child support. Child support is money for the care of kids. Alimony is extra money to the other spouse on a monthly basis to compensate that spouse individually. Kids also implicate the concept of custody—that is, who will take care of them, and when—as well as whether medical decisions involving the kids must be made jointly.

Sometimes, divorce cases go to trial. At trial, a judge hears evidence from each side about where the kids should go and who should get what stuff. If lawyers are the ones presenting that evidence, it can be very expensive—leaving each side with less money to divide up than they started with. Other times, the parties will reach an agreement without having it all decided by a judge, sometimes with the help of a mediator. That agreement needs to be "papered"—that is, someone needs to write up a contract setting forth the terms of the divorce and custody settlement. Usually, that someone is a lawyer, and in some states, the same lawyer cannot represent both people in the marriage. So, a second lawyer becomes involved to review and edit the agreement drafted by the other side's lawyer, which costs more money.

Family law also entails issues like paternity and parental rights, adoption, reproductive technologies, domestic violence, de facto parenthood, and third-party custody—all of which implicate multiple laws of a particular state and, thus, lawyers. Lawyers are hired to explain to clients what the law says. But a good lawyer can do much more. Anyone who has gone through a divorce—either as a spouse or a child of a divorcing couple—knows that it can be one of the more wrenching experiences of life. A good lawyer is more than just an explainer of the law, but also someone who can help a divorcing client develop and execute a strategy that is best for the client and any children involved—all while helping manage the psychological stresses that the process inevitably imposes. Without that kind of lawyer, people can be left twisting in the wind on some of the most critical decisions in life.

I know from personal experience what it feels like to sit in a tight conference room with my ex in another, and a mediator bobbing from room to room in a horse-trading over the most important thing in the world to me: what will become of my children. Mediations involve a third party—usually also a lawyer—who functions to moderate the dispute but who, unlike a judge, does not have the power to make and impose final decisions. In many mediations, one side goes in one room with a lawyer, and the other side goes in the other room with the opposing lawyer. The meditator carries proposals and counter-proposals on how to divide things up back and forth between the two sides, sometimes bringing the couple together to give a snapshot of how the mediator thinks things are going, what the core issues are, and how the mediator thinks things will go in court if the mediation fails and the case goes to trial.

It's important to keep in mind during divorce that if judges ultimately decide the terms of a divorce, then the judges decide them, period. They don't know you or your kids or your ex-partner. Still, their say will likely be the last word, unless their decision is successfully appealed to a higher court. Appeals generally require a showing that the judge got it wrong, not that there was another way to resolve things that was better. And it means even more money spent on litigation. So, all things considered, it's risky to let a judge decide how your family ultimately splits up.

In many states, the "stuff" that's to be divided between a divorcing couple goes 50% to one spouse and 50% to the other, so long as it was accumulated during the marriage. This includes money. Thus, the rules governing how property and other assets will be divided if a judge were to decide a case (somewhat like the rules set forth in the Fourth Amendment for purposes of the *Scott v. Harris* case) is a 50/50 rule. Presumably, this rule would be fairly easy to implement. Make a list of all the assets—the money in bank accounts, the contents of a home, etcetera—and divide it down the middle. But often, that's not how it goes.

For one thing, there's often only "one" of certain things. The antique vase that was given as a wedding gift, the bronzed baby shoes, or the family home. These things need to either be sold, and the proceeds split 50/50 (as often happens with the home, for example), or a numerical value needs to be placed on each of them as a means of dividing things up equally, or each person in the relationship needs to give in to certain demands by giving up certain items that both people really want. This is where value systems come in.

When it comes to custody, many state laws require that judges do what's "in the best interests of the child." This is about as gray as a law can get. Does anyone have a single, black-and-white definition of that concept? Of course not. Some judges might apply a similar 50/50 rule for the custody, such as one week with one parent and one week with another parent. For a twelve-year-old, that is often fine. But for a ten-month-old, less disruption might be preferable. A judge might instead keep the child with a mom (let's assume she was the primary caregiver during the marriage), except for every other weekend, when the child goes with dad. But can we say with certainly that it's always in the best interests of the child to have so little time with dad? No doubt, it depends on the specifics of each family, each parent, and each child. The nuances are too many to identify here. And no judge can know them as well as the parents themselves.

Recall Step 1 of the framework—which is a critical one at the outset of any divorce. Nested within each of the two big issues— that is, what to do about stuff and what to do about custody— are numerous sub-issues, many of which we've already discussed. How much money is there for two homes? How to cover monthly expenses for both parents' households? What is the best school option for a child? And so on.

Step 2 is also vital for divorce, so let's consider that familiar phase of a life cycle in applying that step. Keep in mind, though, that divorce isn't necessarily tragic or even sad—it carries an unfortunate stigma in our society that smacks of defeat and weakness. For many people, it is a positive life event that shows fortitude and even love.

But let's assume for purposes of the framework that a couple is facing an especially painful divorce. As we saw in the introduction to this book, people rely on many hidden biases when they make decisions. Divorces can be so emotionally and psychologically charged that it is virtually impossible for any one parent to be positioned to resolve objectively what's in a child's best interest in relationship with the other parent. This is where the second step in the framework—identifying a hierarchy of values—becomes vital. Even if lawyers are involved, the family's values as well as the personal values of each partner in the relationship won't come from the lawyers involved in the divorce.

How to Identify Your Values

Professor Oyserman again offers a helpful definition: "Values can be thought of as priorities, internal compasses, or springboards for action—moral imperatives." In the first half of the twentieth century, a psychologist named Abraham Maslow did important spadework in identifying the most basic of these with what is now called Maslow's hierarchy of needs. Maslow identified a model of human needs within a pyramid, with physiological needs at the most basic level, then safety, then belongingness and love, then esteem and feelings of accomplishment, and finally self-actualization at the apex.

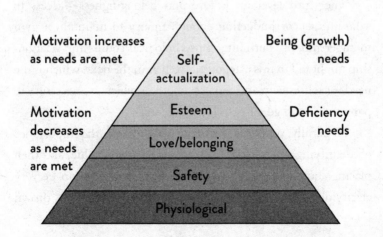

Note that at the very bottom—what makes up the foundation of the pyramid—are physiological needs. These include the basic elements required for life: oxygen, water, food, shelter, clothing, warmth, and sleep. In a situation involving the breakup of a family, this set of values is literally on the negotiation table, or on the judge's bench if matters reach that point. Both spouses—and of course any children—need a roof over their heads and sufficient income to pay for that housing and related utilities, as well as food, clothing, medical care, and transportation to and from work, or perhaps school. Do we really need to focus on the antique vase when we haven't yet figured out how our total combined income will support two households instead of just one?

Maslow goes on to talk about safety needs—the very societal interest that Justice Scalia found important in *Scott v. Harris*—which translate into order and predictability. Making sure that each household is safely and conveniently situated, and that kids have access to adequate childcare, might be the second order of business.

The third level up is love and belongingness—access to a family pet, or budgeting enough money to maintain a gym membership, or continuing a psychological counseling relationship might fall in this category, as well as in the next, which is the need for self-esteem and respect—both of which are necessary to parent well and go on with life in general.

Hopefully, you see what I'm driving at here: the importance of identifying very clearly for yourself what you value, and then placing those values in a hierarchy. This first step can be very clarifying in family life decision-making by helping folks drown out the cacophony of emotionally charged issues and sub-issues that often come into play and allowing surgical strikes at the most vital problems first. It's like hospital triage—a bleeding carotid artery is going to get a doctor's attention before a sprained ankle. Figuring out your own value system can guide complex decision-making in much the same way.

Naming Your Aim

By the same token—and this is important—identifying and prioritizing values can help people let go of the little things and keep their eye on the prize, which in the divorce scenario is usually to move on and find rhythm in life again. Recall that judges usually go 50/50 with money and custody, and whatever they do decide, it's not the family making the final call once a case goes to trial. Yet judges get things wrong. Divorce courts nonetheless remain busy because formal dispute resolution may be the only way to resolve some of the thorniest breakups. But oftentimes, litigation can be avoided.

How? It helps to name your aim.

If you've ever known anyone who is mired in a divorce, you know that there's a lot of hurt. Both sides usually feel wounded after years of commitment and even sacrifice and want to walk away feeling whole. People understandably want to move on with as little change as possible too. They want the same quality of life that can come from a two-income household, or one in which the kids have a full-time parent at home. They will hold out for what they believe is fair or right, which often leads to litigation, which leads to drained bank accounts. Ultimately, a judge might apply the 50/50 rule anyway, with less to divide up.

Naming your aim is a recognition that giving up on a strong belief that "I deserve more," or "I deserve x, y, and z," might be worth it to serve a value of greater priority. If the aim is to get on with life as quickly as possible and with as little money spent on attorneys' fees as possible, for example, then the antique vase seems less important. If the budget shows that another $5,000 on attorneys' fees means that a highly prized value—like maybe a vacation once a year with the kids—goes away, then it might be easier to cut bait and sign a deal that doesn't feel just right.

Before moving on, let me offer another analogy I embraced a few years ago, and which I find myself returning to again and again: the Taoist symbol of yin and yang.

When asked what they want for themselves and their kids, many people dealing with a tough family life situation might answer, "I just want to be happy." Of course, that's unrealistic as a constant state of being. Nobody is happy every moment of their lives. Think instead of the two halves of the yin and yang sphere as "order" and "chaos"—both of which are inevitable parts of life. Too much chaos—or seeing everything in all black—is unsustainable. We lose our minds. Too much order—or all white—is like a grape dying on the vine. Life becomes boring and, well, lifeless. The ideal state is enough order with enough chaos to make life interesting and enough chaos with enough order that we don't dip underwater and drown. In a perfect divorce, there's a little black and a little white for each party. Understanding that aim from the onset can save a lot of heartache and money.

Noticing Your Audience

We've been spending some time on divorce and custody questions and how judges might think about those decisions. Most family life decisions are not made by judges, of course. Lawyers understand that identifying the audience is an important aspect of decision-making. Convincing a judge to rule in your client's favor is a very different task than convincing a client to take a particular course of action. In family life, deciding whether to have a child is different from deciding how to deal with a child in tricky parenting situations. The framework can be applied in those situations too.

Consider something as basic as deciding what to do with a difficult teenager. When I say "difficult," I don't mean to suggest that the hypothetical teen is anything but perfectly ordinary. Teen brains are not yet fully wired, and they tend to make decisions reactively and on impulse, which can make trying to reason with them frustrating and stressful. But suppose, for example, that your fifteen-year-old wants to pierce her tongue. As a parent, your immediate instinct is probably to protect her—tier two on Maslow's hierarchy of needs. But let's not forget the very bottom rung of the pyramid in this moment. Does a piercing affect the basic necessities of the child's life? Probably not. And it might actually serve her sense of belonging, which is tier three, and her self-esteem, tier four. This is not to say that she gets her piercing—just that identifying and prioritizing your values as a parent is a useful first step in deciding how to deal with the situation.

Naming your aim—which might be to keep her safe while ensuring that she grows wings strong enough to fly on her own—clarifies what's the best outcome for you as a parent, which might at first have been a resounding "no" to the piercing. After applying this step of the framework, you might come to realize that the aim is much bigger and more nuanced than that, so it becomes easier to let go of your knee-jerk desire to protect. If you have a spouse, that person might need to name an aim and key values in this situation too. Depending on how your partner was raised, the list might be different from yours, and some discussion could be in order before proceeding.

Finally, reminding yourself that your audience is a child of fifteen—not an adult with full brain development and life experience—could help you moderate how you approach both the decision and the methods by which you communicate with her about it. Parenting is super hard, and all parents make mistakes—even the best ones. At the very least, Step 1 of the lawyering framework could help move a hard family decision from the realm of mostly emotion to one that's more cognitive (and yes, lawyerly). Just like in actual lawyering, identifying values and aims can put you in greater control of the decision from the get-go.

We will return to this step of the framework throughout the book.

STEP 2 CHECKLIST: VALUES AND AIMS

✓ First, apply Step 1 by identifying the issues and sub-issues involved in the decision.

✓ Next, identify the general category of the decision you are making (e.g., family life, civic life, health care, work, information consumption, hiring a lawyer).

✓ List what values matter to you around this topic (e.g., expenditure of resources, time, energy; relationship with ____; family harmony; benevolence; engaging with others including ____; hard work; skill development such as ____; thrift; education; industriousness; honesty; helping others; individualism; social justice; personal freedom; group harmony; personal happiness; duty; beauty; religious doctrine; honesty; forgiveness of ____; benevolence; excitement; conformity to ____; tradition; security; financial gain; physical survival; social interchange; continuity; achievement; stimulation; hedonism; power; fairness; caring; loyalty to ____; acceptance of authority; patriotism; humility; self-respect; admiration; fame).

✓ What are the top three to five values of yours that matter for this decision (in order of importance)?

✓ Who is your audience?

✓ In light of your values and your audience, what is your ultimate aim in making this decision?

3

Thinking Like a
Lawyer in Civic Life

Ask not what your country can do for you; ask what
you can do for your country.
—John F. Kennedy

Have you ever found yourself on a jury facing confusing legalese
and competing stories of what may have happened? Or maybe
you want to make a bigger difference in your community—
through volunteering, recreational sports teams, or group membership (e.g., the PTA or a book club)—and don't know how
best to start that process. Or perhaps you could just use some
help managing phone calls and door-to-door financial solicita-
tions that come your way. How do you decide which requests are
legitimate and which are not?

Civic life captures a range of activities, but the defining fea-
ture is engagement with others in a broader community rather
than exclusively within your private life. Voting is perhaps the
most foundational aspect of civic life in the United States. It is
the means by which "We the People" hire and fire government

officials. Politicians hold significant power over civilians, but not through some divine grace or birthright. Voters give them their jobs at the ballot box. Yet no single voter can choose elected officials—it only happens in great numbers. Thus, it's the very definition of community engagement.

America weathered a bruising election in 2020, with record voter turnout across the political spectrum, massive protests around issues of social justice, and escalations of violence in the streets. Some people came away from that year turned off from voting altogether, believing that the election system is completely broken. Others are deeply concerned about how polarized public discourse is these days. It is so full of misinformation that merely establishing baseline facts has become a real challenge. How do you go about getting good and accurate information about a candidate or an issue? How do you decide whether to vote at all? And if you do decide to engage in civic life at the ballot box, how do you make sure that you are actually voting for your own interests—and not those of some big corporation or political machine operating behind the scenes? Maybe you want to really jump into the fray and run for office—how do you go about doing that?

In modern times, misinformation has become an exceedingly difficult problem to tackle. A few decades ago, news and facts came from a handful of sources: major television networks (CBS News, ABC News, NBC News, PBS News), a few newspapers (*New York Times, Wall Street Journal, Washington Post*, your local paper), the local library's card catalogue of books, established magazines like *Time* and *Life*, and maybe a home encyclopedia. Growing up in Buffalo, New York, in the 1970s and 1980s, my family had two main grocery stores to choose from—Bells and Super Duper. My mom went to Super Duper for a while because it was giving away a new encyclopedia volume each month. I was one of five kids, and we had a lot of school projects between us, so this was a valuable resource. The dog-eared, outdated Super Duper encyclopedia was our go-to source for "good" information for years. It's just incredible to think about that now.

Today, of course, we have cyberspace and smartphones. The big online companies Google, Amazon, Microsoft, and Facebook are estimated to hold at least 1,200 petabytes of information between them. It would take you 2.5 years of non-stop binge-watching full-length movies to get through a single petabyte, which is equal to 1,000,000 gigabytes of storage data. If you loaded 1 petabyte on 1 gigabyte flash drives and lined them all up, it would span 92 football fields. Now multiply that by 1,200— and that only accounts for the data held by the four largest companies. It doesn't include data held by governments, universities, and smaller players like Dropbox.

Now think about the "phone" you carry around in your pocket or purse. "Phone" is actually a misnomer, as your smartphone does much more than transmit voices over a distance using wire or radio like they did when I was a kid. Your phone is more powerful than IBM's mainframe computer that NASA used to send Apollo missions to the moon in the 1960s. Its circuitry could translate the equivalent of one novel per minute, while most desktop computers today have six times that capacity. Compared to today's laptops, the IBM System/360 computer analyzed and transmitted less information to the Apollo flight controllers to enable the first landing on the moon and the lift-off data needed by astronauts Neil Armstrong and Edwin "Buzz" Aldrin to reconnect with a command module and return to Earth.

Figuring out how to collect and process the tsunami of information we have at our fingertips is a task that our brains have not yet figured out how to do effectively. The first flight computers came on the scene in the 1960s. In six decades—less than an average lifespan by today's standards—a longstanding human need for finding basic information has shifted to a human need for figuring out how to sort information into the basic and the extraneous or even false. Yet how to manage information overload is not something that our children are learning how to do well in modern schools—let alone the millions of adults who grew up with pen and pencil, not apps, avatars, and virtual workplaces.

One of the foundational skills of lawyering is gathering lots of information and sorting through it effectively. Here again is our B-I-C-A-T framework for legal decision-making:

1. **Break** the problem down.
2. **Identify** your values and your aim.
3. **Collect** lots of knowledge.
4. **Argue** both sides of each point.
5. **Tolerate** the fact that people will disagree with your choice—and that you might feel conflicted.

In this chapter, we focus on **Step 3: Collect lots of knowledge on both sides of each point.** By knowledge, I mostly mean facts. For lawyers, facts can mean a narrative or story—the "once upon a time" tale that led two parties to begin a dispute that mushroomed into a lawsuit. Often, there are two sides to that story.

Lawyers in the United States unpack the story during a legal process called discovery—they exchange relevant documents and talk to witnesses. Once the documents and witnesses are winnowed down, the best stuff is presented at trial. At that point, we call the information "evidence," and there are rules that judges must apply to decide which pieces of evidence are acceptable at trial and which are not.

The rules of evidence are a big reason why courts are fundamentally different from politicians. Politicians can say things—even if untrue—so long as they get away with it in the court of public opinion. If other powerful people don't call them out, or if the public is led to believe things that aren't true, then falsehoods simply carry the day. Judges don't have that option—if they allow bad information to get before a jury for political reasons, they can be reversed by a higher appeals court. Judges hate that because it means they have to start over again. So, the rules of the game generally keep judges honest.

For lawyers, the other primary category of information is what we call "law." A law is a rule that is backed by some form of government authority. The U.S. Constitution is a law. Statutes passed by legislatures are laws. What people call "regulations" are laws too—even though they are not passed by legislatures. They are passed by agencies. At the federal level, those agencies answer to the president—not directly to lawmakers. The last big category of law is what we call common law, or judge-made law. We've discussed common law in this book already—it's the outcome of a prior case that lawyers and judges use to compare and contrast to a new case. I called this the "me too!" and "not it!" formula that lawyers use to either piggyback on a prior case because its outcome would be good for a client, or to distinguish a prior case that had an outcome that would be bad for a client in order to persuade a judge to rule the other way this time.

Applying Step 3

The closest overlap between regular civic life and the work of a lawyer is probably jury duty. Juries are a cross-section of regular people who are called upon by the government to decide cases that are brought to trial. There are two kinds of juries in the United States—grand juries, which decide whether to charge a party with a crime, and petit juries. Petit juries are the ones that actually hear the evidence at a trial and decide whether defendants did what they're accused of doing and, in many cases, whether they should go to jail. In civil cases brought between two private parties, petit juries also resolve disputes that result in an award of money damages that one side must pay to the other side.

Juries are special for several reasons. First, they are comprised of laypeople rather than politicians, bureaucrats, or judges—people who are sometimes pejoratively deemed "elites." Expertise is helpful, but the theory behind juries is that common sense and consensus can produce fairer outcomes. Jurors bring their personal experiences to a story—and don't primarily rely on the legal nuances and distinctions that may otherwise distract lawyers and judges.

Second, jurors deliberate in secret and don't have to give their reasons for a decision. Judges must put their rationales on the record somehow so an appeals court can decide if they did the right thing. The U.S. Supreme Court routinely (but not always) gives reasons for its decisions so that lower courts can know how to apply the same or similar laws in the future. But for the same reasons that they're heralded, juries have been criticized—arguably, the jury system enables amateurs to decide questions as substantial as whether a Fortune 500 company violated complex security rules and whether a man should lose his life for a crime that he claims he did not commit.

Given the gravity of the work of a juror, how do you go about the exercise of jury duty if—like most of us—you are called to do it? In most states, lawyers are struck from serving on juries by counsel who do not want them to hijack the conversation when the other jurors deliberate. If you haven't been to law school, the B-I-C-A-T framework can help get you through jury duty with confidence that you applied your own common sense with diligence and integrity. As we will discuss in this chapter, the key is to listen hard for both sides of the story, and to identify the rules—or laws—that govern the outcome. Usually, the judge will give these to jurors in the form of jury instructions, but as I tell my students, much of the law is just a crystallization of some combination of common-sense ideas like fairness, accuracy, and efficiency. You have those at your disposal already.

I was on a couple of juries while living in Washington, D.C. (Although lawyers rarely get chosen for juries, D.C. has a high concentration of lawyers, so people with law degrees inevitably do.) One case involved a criminal charge against a man for driving without a license in a parking lot. The apparent back story was that the man was a lookout for other criminal activity. Prosecutors sought to break up the scheme by going after the lookout. The evidence presented involved the testimony of a police officer and nothing more. The defendant did not testify; nor did any of the other individuals who were present at the incident and presumably knew the defendant. The jury could not decide unanimously that he was guilty, which is the requirement for a criminal conviction, so he was released. Basically, a couple of the jurors had bad experiences with police officers and believed that they were mostly corrupt and prone to lying. They weren't willing to trust the evidence on behalf of the government.

The other jury I was on involved a civil case for money damages against a car wash. The plaintiff was driving through a car wash when her windshield cracked and collapsed. She claimed that the incident was the result of something defective in the car wash, although her lawyer didn't attempt to explain what that defect was. She just argued that this kind of thing doesn't happen under normal circumstances, so it must be the car wash's fault. The jury rendered a decision for the car wash, in part because the driver was not claiming physical injuries—only emotional injuries that she alleged entitled her to a money payment from the car wash. During her testimony, the lawyer for the car wash revealed that she had a terrible highway accident only a few months earlier, whereby her car was flipped upside down, injuring her neck. The lawyer asked her on the witness stand whether it was possible that her emotional stress was in fact caused by that incident—not the car wash accident. She said no, but the jury was unconvinced.

As I'll explain later, there are two primary categories of information that these scenarios implicate: the facts and the law. There are usually two sides of the story when it comes to facts that go before a jury. If the story is hopelessly one-sided, a judge will get rid of a civil case without sending it to a jury on the theory that it's a waste of time. This is what happened in the *Scott v. Harris* case we discussed earlier. Not necessarily so with criminal cases, which mostly hinge on whether a prosecutor or grand jury decides that there is enough evidence against a defendant to warrant bringing a case in the first place. In the criminal case I sat on as juror, there weren't really two sides to the story offered. There was one version of the facts presented at trial: the lookout guy drove a car without a license. That was probably enough to convict, because there was no evidence weighing against it. But the full jury didn't believe that side. It came down to the credibility of the police officer.

In the civil case against the car wash, there were two sides presented, but the plaintiff's story didn't persuade the jury. The civil case also failed because of a wrinkle under the law: The car wash couldn't be liable for the plaintiff's emotional injuries that it didn't actually cause. Even if the car wash caused her windshield to crack, she couldn't win unless that error harmed her in the way she claimed—by hurting her emotionally. The car accident caused that, or so the jury decided.

When lawyers get a new problem, they immediately go to work identifying the laws that might be relevant. They also take pains to uncover the underlying story, or the "facts"—as well as the places within the story where people might disagree on what actually happened. You need to do the same thing when thinking like a lawyer at home or at work.

Let's consider this imaginary case: Loretta's car is hit on the passenger side by Maria's car. The accident occurs at an intersection with a traffic light. Loretta claims that the light was green when she went through the intersection, and that Maria was running a red light in the opposite direction when she hit Loretta's car. Maria claims that her light was green, and that Loretta was the one running a red light when Maria mistakenly hit Loretta's car. Because Loretta had run her red light, Maria maintains, the collision wasn't Maria's fault. So, there are two possible narratives here. Each witness tells one version of a story as to what happened.

Imagine that Loretta hires a lawyer to sue Maria. The first thing the lawyer would do is identify the law that applies—here, it's the law of negligence, among other possible things. Negligence law requires drivers to act with due care when driving. If they don't, they can be liable for money damages. The lawyer will also dig into the facts and try to collect knowledge around what really happened. The lawyer will interview Loretta first, and later ask to talk to Maria in a deposition. Counsel will also talk to any witnesses on the scene, find out if there were hidden cameras that might have captured the incident, and perhaps look at the police report (if one exists).

Although Loretta's lawyer wants to achieve the outcome the client wants—presumably, getting money from Maria to have her car fixed and maybe pay some medical bills—the lawyer knows that there's a need to uncover both sides of the story first. In her anger and frustration over the accident, Loretta might not have told the lawyer that she wasn't wearing her glasses that day, although she's nearsighted. The lawyer needs to know this. All the good, the bad, and the ugly must come out as soon as possible to her lawyer—because it will come out eventually. It's a nightmare to be blindsided at trial. And because the law confines judges' ability to make rulings based on bias or politics, the bad facts will ultimately hurt Loretta's case.

"My-Side" Bias

Think about this lawyerly approach to facts for a moment. It's probably fairly different from how many of us make decisions in our everyday lives. When faced with a personal dilemma, we aren't always naturally inclined to dig up both sides of a story. Psychologists call this "confirmation bias," and it often gets in the way of getting an accurate picture of things. As I mentioned in the introduction to this book, confirmation bias is the tendency to look for information that reinforces what we already believe, and it can be accompanied by the refusal to listen to facts that contradict our beliefs.

We tend to follow the social media accounts of people who say things that make sense to us. And we might not follow the accounts of people who say things on the opposite side of an issue. The same goes with what kind of news we read. We might only click on or tune into news sites that we know will confirm our point of view. The other side never gets our attention because we don't seek it out. As a result, the "truth" can amount to a one-sided version of facts that are carefully (albeit inadvertently) chosen to correspond to an existing set of beliefs.

This lack of curiosity about the other side of the story happens a lot in everyday life. A friend is sure that his spouse is cheating. As "proof," he points to her lack of interest in him at the end of a workday, or the fact that she's constantly on her phone and sometimes chuckles when reading texts, which he assumes is because she's flirting with someone else. A co-worker sends an email to your boss. When she doesn't get a reply for a couple of days, she reads the lack of response as confirmation that the boss doesn't like her. This can work in the other direction too. The boss might have passed your co-worker over for a promotion because he assumes that a working mother of young children won't be willing or able to handle the extra stress that the new job entails. But of course, there are many other possible explanations for each of these scenarios.

This "my-side" bias is entirely normal, but it doesn't necessarily produce the best decisions—particularly in complex, risky situations. We act on it because it's less taxing to us cognitively than pulling apart every issue, diving into it, and then arriving at an independent conclusion. It also just feels better than entertaining an opposing view, which can sting and hurt one's self-esteem because it challenges what we believed to be true. None of this is done consciously, which is why it's important to identify the phenomenon of confirmation bias so we can catch and outmaneuver it when it might matter. If hearing out the other side could lead to a better decision on an issue that we really care about, then practicing Step 3 in the B-I-C-A-T framework is worth the extra effort.

In making civic life decisions, collecting lots of information is also very important—both in terms of what laws might apply and identifying the key facts and validating their accuracy. But what *are* facts in the first place? It's easy to get into a theoretical debate over this question. Is it a fact that eating meat is bad? Or is that opinion? What about whether the planet is warming? Or to make the question even more complicated, what about whether the planet is warming due to the activity of humans? Is the answer to that a fact or an opinion?

People often confuse facts with opinions. The planet is warming—that's factually established by science. There is also scientific evidence that the planet is warming due to human activity. Debate also exists over what to do about climate change—whether regulating fossil fuels would ultimately help or hurt the job market, for example. But that doesn't change the facts.

Perhaps amazingly, lawyers and judges working in the profession rarely, if ever, get into this kind of debate. The question for lawyers isn't whether a fact is a fact, but whether a fact is reliable—and thus useful. Assume again that Maria and Loretta each testify that they recall their respective lights being green. But it can't be both ways—one light was green, and one was red. Which version of the story is "fact"? Or put another way, which woman is telling the "truth"? In law, lawyers will look for more authoritative evidence—like a video of the incident showing which light was green, or perhaps a municipal record of the timing of the light changes at the intersection that day.

Without that kind of hard evidence, a jury might be left to decide which witness to believe. But if one side of the story has no legitimate factual basis—if Maria, for example, testified that the light "must have been green" because she "never runs red lights," the judge won't let the jury hear her side of the story. Only Loretta's will be heard. The law usually won't entertain guesses or speculation or fantasy.

Of course, even with good information, sometimes jurors get it wrong. As of September 2019, for example, a whopping 167 people on death row were exonerated by DNA evidence collected from blood, hair, or skin cells at the scene of a crime. This means they were wrongly convicted by human beings on juries.

That kind of scientific evidence doesn't lie. The juries in those 167 cases just got the facts wrong. But even in cases where jurors got it wrong, lawyers tried hard to present both sides of the story.

Here's the thing to keep firmly in mind: A good lawyer *always* looks for both sides of a story. Overcoming confirmation bias is inherently built into the law school curriculum. Lawyers might represent clients whom they know are guilty of a crime. They know that the other side of the story is the truth. For a guilty client, a lawyer will argue that the government doesn't have its factual scenario buttoned down—that it can't meet its burden of proof. To do that effectively, the defense lawyer must know where all the problems are for a client's case. Defense lawyers have to be able to articulate the other side of the story seamlessly.

In everyday life, we get things wrong too. But ideally, when it comes to big decisions, gathering as many facts as possible is an important step to making the best decision possible. This means getting facts out on both sides of the story. We will return to the "both sides" concept in the next chapter—it's *that* important to good thinking. For now, let's focus on getting the relevant information on the table in the first place.

A Law School Lesson: *Hickman v. Taylor*

How Do Both Sides of the Story Come Out in Legal Cases?

Hickman v. Taylor is yet another important case that every law student reads. It established what's known as the "work product doctrine," which attorneys use to shield certain information from the other side. I know I just said that good lawyers work to unearth all the relevant facts bearing on a case, both good and bad. But some information can be kept confidential, for various reasons.

Hickman v. Taylor established that lawyers don't have to give the other side their notes about the strategy for winning a case—that would be unfair and create a disincentive to write anything down. If football coaches knew that the opposing team could get their game plans so long as they're written down, they wouldn't ever write them down. Same goes for lawyers. If the other side could get a lawyer's notes on which witnesses to call at trial, for example, lawyers wouldn't bother writing things down about their trial strategies because it could be used against them and their clients. *Hickman v. Taylor* assumes this wouldn't be a great thing for clients and the legal system. It would be a problem if lawyers had to rely solely on memory in representing clients—they'd make avoidable mistakes, and chaos could ensue in many corners of the legal system.

For our purposes, *Hickman v. Taylor* is a helpful case for teasing out how to identify the range of knowledge—both facts and the governing rules—that bears on a decision you are facing. Here's the story.

On February 7, 1943, a tugboat called the *J. M. Taylor* sank when helping to tow a barge across the Delaware River in Philadelphia. The wooden barge was one of two owned by the Baltimore & Ohio (B&O) Railroad. The night before, the two barges had sunk, got stuck in a riverbed, and were left overnight. The tugboat remained moored to the sunken and stuck barges. One of the two barges became dislodged, floated to the surface, and struck the tugboat. Then the tugboat sank. Five out of nine crew members on the tugboat drowned, including a man by the name of Norman E. Hickman. Three days later, the tugboat owners and their insurance company hired a lawyer by the name of Samuel B. Fortenbaugh, Jr. Why? Because they knew they were about to get sued.

Imagine that you are Mr. Fortenbaugh. Your goal is to minimize your clients' liability for having to pay money to the families of the five dead crew members. What facts do you want to learn more about? Here's a starter list:

- What caused the accident?
    - Who was driving the tugboat?
    - Was there any underlying problem with the tugboat itself?
    - Was there a problem with the barge owned by the B&O Railroad?
    - What were the weather conditions on the day of the incident?
- Was any other vessel involved in the accident?
- Did the surviving crew members suffer any injuries?
- How to quantify the financial losses to the families of the deceased?
- Was the tugboat damaged?

These are all questions of fact—what happened on that fateful February day. But Fortenbaugh was pondering questions of law, too, when he first sat down to work on this case. What were the rules that governed tugboat-driven barge crossings? Those rules would dictate who was responsible for the accident and thus for compensating the victims.

We've already heard of one such rule: the law of negligence. In this case, people had a duty to exercise reasonable care in preparing barges for transport across a river and in providing a tugboat to aid in that effort. The folks driving the tugboat needed to exercise reasonable care, too. So Fortenbaugh knew that he needed to identify all the potential pitfalls in his clients' case. Were there any facts suggesting that his clients, the tugboat owners, failed to exercise reasonable care? Because if so, then they might have wound up having to pay out settlements to the deceased crew members' families or face a high jury verdict, and Fortenbaugh had to strategize around that possibility.

Fortenbaugh would ask the same question of the B&O Railroad. If the facts showed that there was something wrong with the barge, then Fortenbaugh might have been able to point the legal finger at B&O, a third party. In fact, Fortenbaugh might have had grounds to sue B&O for damages to his clients' tugboat. This wouldn't necessarily have erased the tugboat owners' liability to the families, but it could have softened the blow.

So, now we have a set of factual questions and a set of legal questions. The facts will drive how the legal issues resolve, specifically whether the ultimate blame is placed on the tugboat company or someone else. Hopefully, that is evident from our discussion so far.

The next question is: If you were Fortenbaugh, how would you go about gathering facts to find out answers to the questions you identified? Remember, Fortenbaugh needs to know about the harmful facts just as much as he needs to uncover whatever facts are helpful to his clients' case. A harmful fact might be, for example, that the tugboat was sloppily moored to the sunken barge, rather than to an anchor, which is more secure and thus the better way to moor a tugboat. It turns out that the tugboat operators didn't sound any alarm overnight, either, which could have drawn assistance for the accident before the sunken barge became dislodged and hit the tugboat. These are the kinds of facts that would have gotten Fortenbaugh to think hard about whether it would have been better for his clients to pay some damages out of court rather than put the sad story before a jury.

In 1943, there were two primary sources of facts in litigation: documents and witness testimony. (These days, lawyers start with an internet search, but that was the stuff of science fiction back then.) If you were Fortenbaugh, where might you start? If you're thinking that you'd talk to witnesses, then you're already thinking like a lawyer—because that's just what Fortenbaugh did. You might also want to get documents relating to the care and maintenance of the tugboat and the barge, but the latter is the kind of thing that Fortenbaugh probably couldn't easily get from B&O without filing a lawsuit, which would have allowed him to force the railroad to turn over relevant information.

Fortenbaugh privately interviewed the survivors and took written statements from them. On March 29, the survivors signed their statements. He also interviewed other people who might have had information relating to the accident and drew up memoranda memorializing what they told him. Later, claims were made in court against the tugboat owners by representatives of all five deceased crew members. Four were settled out of court.

The last holdout—the estate of Mr. Hickman—continued with its suit against the tugboat owners for money damages.

This is where things got interesting—and novel—when it came to Fortenbaugh's foresight in gathering facts in the weeks immediately after the accident. It's easy to understand why he did this quickly—memories fade, so talking to witnesses as soon as possible was probably the best way to get the most complete recollections possible. Also, Fortenbaugh was able to get the lay of the land enough to settle four of the five cases. The good, bad, and the ugly were important to know so that he could evaluate the possible price tag for his clients if a case ever went to verdict.

Lawyers for the Hickman estate agreed that Fortenbaugh had done his homework—and well. Once the lawsuit was filed, and the fact-gathering process of discovery began, they asked for "exact copies" of Fortenbaugh's written witness statements. For good measure, the lawyers also demanded that if any witness interviews were merely oral, Fortenbaugh "set forth in detail the exact provisions of any such oral statements or reports." In other words, they wanted Fortenbaugh to do their work for them—a classic freeloader problem.

If you've ever heard the story of *The Little Red Hen*, you know what a freeloader is. Dating from 1874, it tells the tale of a red hen who decides to make bread. She works hard to plant and harvest wheat and grind it into flour before baking it into bread. At each stage, she asks the other animals on the farm for help, and they refuse, making excuses for their laziness. When the bread is out of the oven and slathered with butter, the other animals are more than happy to have a slice, but the little red hen refuses to allow them to freeload off her work. If they wanted bread, they should have helped make it.

Fortenbaugh probably felt just like the little red hen. He had taken steps to interview witnesses immediately after the action. Hickman's lawyers did not, even though they presumably had just as much of a chance. Moreover, Fortenbaugh probably knew that the kinds of questions he asked the witnesses, and the responses he chose to memorialize in writing, could give his opponents insight into how Fortenbaugh viewed the strengths and weaknesses of his clients' case. In the American legal system, if you don't ask the right questions, it's too bad for you—witnesses are not required to volunteer information to lawyers, although they should volunteer everything if they're speaking to their *own* counsel. Hence, how Fortenbaugh conducted his interviews was valuable information.

The problem for Fortenbaugh was that the rules that applied at that point in time to the discovery process didn't allow him to keep the witness statements confidential. The American legal system is premised on the notion that it's best to put all relevant information on the table—so long as an opponent asks for it—because that way, the outcome will be based on the fullest picture of what actually happened and thus reveal as accurately and fairly as possible who is responsible for any injuries. Still, there are a handful of what I call "gatekeepers" of discovery—rules that allow parties to keep certain information off-limits. One is relevance. If Hickman's estate had asked Fortenbaugh for information about a slip-and-fall accident that occurred in the tugboat owners' main office three years prior, Fortenbaugh could have refused. That information bears no relevance whatsoever to what happened with the drowning incident.

A second gatekeeper has to do with burden—if a request is overly burdensome for no real benefit, a party can refuse. If the Hickman estate asked Fortenbaugh for copies of every customer file since the beginning of the tugboat company's existence (the company was called Taylor and Anderson Towing and Lighterage Company), that might turn up some relevant information—such as another incident where a customer complained about tugboat employees failing to properly moor a boat, for example. But the off-chance of finding that needle in a haystack would be outweighed by the burden of making exact copies of all those years' worth of files. But when it came to copying a few witness statements, Fortenbaugh didn't have a burdensomeness argument.

The third option is known as the attorney-client privilege. When clients communicate with their attorneys about legal questions confidentially, that information is protected from an opponent. (Keep in mind that this does not mean that talking to a lawyer about anything is privileged—the communication must be about a legal issue, and it must be secret. These caveats are widely misunderstood.) The idea behind the attorney-client privilege is, once again, to create an incentive for lawyers to write things down—and for clients to confide in lawyers. Neither would happen if any and every conversation with a lawyer about legal advice was fair game to adversaries. But the witnesses to the accident weren't Fortenbaugh's clients. The tugboat owners were. He couldn't use the attorney-client privilege to keep the witness statements from the Hickman estate's lawyers, because the privilege simply did not apply.

Nonetheless, Fortenbaugh stood on principle and refused to

turn over the statements. He had no legal rule that gave him the authority to do that—he just believed that it wasn't fair to him or his clients to let the Hickman estate freeload on his work. The judge ordered him to turn the material over, and he still refused. The judge reacted to his defiance by holding him in contempt— meaning he put Fortenbaugh in jail. That's how dedicated Mr. Fortenbaugh was to his clients and the cause of justice!

The decision was appealed all the way to the U.S. Supreme Court, which held that Fortenbaugh was right in refusing to comply with the Hickman estate's request. The Court made up a brand-new rule in doing so, which we now call the "work product doctrine." Basically, in addition to the three gatekeepers described previously, if lawyers are taking notes in anticipation of litigation or a trial, those notes can be kept confidential. There are nuances to the doctrine, but that's the gist of it.

I hope it's clear by now how important it is to get both sides of a story in the law. Fortenbaugh was willing to go to jail to protect the facts and notes he had collected before his client was sued. You can also see how lawyers go about excavating facts—they look for questions, not answers. Once they have a list of questions, they get curious about who might know anything about the questions, either through their own personal experiences or by virtue of documents found in file cabinets or, in modern times, on a hard drive or in the cloud.

Hickman v. Taylor underscores the importance of identifying the decision on the table (e.g., who is responsible for the five deaths and damage to the tugboat), the factual questions that need asking in order to answer that overarching question (e.g., did the tugboat employees moor the tugboat to the sunken barge), and what rules apply (e.g., the law of negligence and the gatekeepers to discovery). If you ever wind up on a jury, you can use this checklist to figure out how to manage the process—identify the relevant facts on both sides, the relevant laws governing the case, and decide which version is better supported by verifiable evidence.

Now let's apply these tools to some of the other questions that arise in civic life: donating, volunteering, group membership, voting, and running for office. In that process, we will explore another topic that Mr. Fortenbaugh didn't have to contend with because the *Hickman v. Taylor* case was not about evidence at trial (which had not occurred yet): assessing the validity and legitimacy of the avalanche of information we get through our laptops and smartphones.

Collecting Lots of Facts

Let's begin with something very basic, like volunteering in your community, at your kids' school, or for a national organization. Deciding to volunteer can feel a bit daunting, for several reasons. It might push you out of your routine and maybe even beyond your comfort zone. If a friend doesn't loop you into an opportunity, it can feel fairly intimidating to cold call an organization and just show up one day—kind of like the first day at a new school when you were a kid.

It's also hard to discern whether the work you will be doing will be meaningful to you. Sorting used clothes for a homeless shelter could be very rewarding for some people, but less so for others. If you have a special skill like accounting or marketing, you might prefer to look for that kind of opportunity as a volunteer, but that might require a greater commitment to the organization than you are comfortable making right now.

Maybe you're not sure how you can help but are intrigued by the mission of an organization you saw on a neighborhood listserv. You show up at an information session only to leave confused as to next steps. Nobody follows up with you afterwards. You wind up thinking that it's not worth your time to hunt-and-peck at volunteering options after all, and wind up doing nothing about it. Six months later, you feel bad that you haven't managed to find a service opportunity, knowing it's something you'd ideally like to do. How can the B-I-C-A-T framework assist with this process?

Well, for starters, there are Steps 1 and 2 in the framework to contend with. First, break the problem down. Then, identify your values and your aim. Breaking the problem down might look something like this:

> Goals in volunteering
> Time and other logistical constraints

From there, you might identify sub-categories. For goals, it could be making an impact, meeting new people, building a network, and maybe even just feeling good. Research shows that regularly volunteering can help you live longer, help with depression, and stave off disease. Studies of 2,000 people over a five-year period also showed that those who volunteered 5.8 hours per month or more were happier overall. Why that is so isn't altogether clear, but it could be some combination of social interaction, physical activity, and a neurochemical reward in the brain that comes from helping others. Elderly individuals who volunteered at least 200 hours per year lowered their risk of heart disease by 40%. Chronic pain sufferers who peer-volunteered reported reduced symptoms of their own pain. Sociologists have concluded that teen volunteering contributes to higher grades and increased self-esteem.

Volunteering also pays forward—research shows that others are likely to come along with you. It's not just your contribution to the public good that you should consider, therefore, but also the ripple effects that your service might have on others. You are probably not the only person you know who is inclined to volunteer but could use the influence of someone else to get over the hump.

Your aim under Step 2 might include finding a way to use certain skills that you already have. Perhaps your day job is behind a computer, and you really want physical activity on the weekends. Or you crunch numbers for a living but have a knack for art or music and would like to find a volunteer opportunity that gets that part of your brain working. Thinking deliberately and consciously about these issues—and affirmatively listing them—will help get you closer to a decision that works for you.

The second sub-category—timing and other logistics—entails issues like whether you already have a paid job that takes priority, the hourly commitment for that work, whether you have children that may or may not be in a position to join you in the effort, whether you have access to transportation to an offsite volunteer job, and so on. Some volunteer opportunities can be met from your home computer or smartphone—such as staffing a hotline for people in need or canvassing voters for a candidate for office. For this step, list all the relevant issues in play. When you're finished, circle the heart (or hearts) of the matter for you, as we discussed in the first chapter of the book.

Step 2 is fairly important when it comes to volunteering: identifying your values and naming your aim. The second part of this is a bit redundant with Step 1 under our analysis—that is, you have already identified your goals. You know that it's not about paying the bills, for instance. The "values" piece, however, is significant here. There are literally hundreds—if not thousands—of non-profit organizations that need financial assistance, and giving money can be a very meaningful way to contribute, although perhaps not one that translates into the benefits to well-being that come from actively devoting hours to a cause. Whatever the objective, making a list of the social values that matter to you is probably a worthwhile exercise. Perhaps it's race equality, food security, respect for animals, environmental sustainability, literacy, education, or public health. Take a good half hour to sit with the various options and see what gets you excited. From this list, circle three to five values that are in the top tier for you—chances are, if you make a difference regarding those values, the health benefits to volunteering will come through for you.

The initial part of Step 3 is to collect facts. What does this mean? Once you have figured out what areas you want to make a difference in, you need to get online and research the non-profit organizations that work in that area. Maybe you decide to focus on the elderly and end-of-life support. Steps 1 and 2 got you to that threshold. Step 3 is the place to do the research into the organizations that offer volunteer opportunities in this area.

Imagine you do an internet search and identify a few national organizations such as AARP and Meals on Wheels, as well as some local retirement communities and hospitals that accept volunteer help. The fact-finding step means researching each of these based on the priorities you identified in Steps 1 and 2. Narrow the options down based on the skills needed and hours available in your schedule, for example. Then give the organizations a call to pose whatever related questions come up for you. Maybe ask if you can talk to someone who is already working as a volunteer to see if the job expectations line up with what you're looking for. You can also ask that person the hard questions—the good, the bad, and the ugly, like Mr. Fortenbaugh did when he interviewed witnesses in the *Hickman v. Taylor* case—so that you can be fully informed when you decide where to give your time.

At this point, let's take a moment to pause and consider whether the framework has produced a different kind of decision-making process than you might have employed prior to reading this book. We've now applied the first three steps. Hopefully, you can see how decision-makers are in a much more focused and thoughtful place than they would be if they just opened a browser and typed in "volunteer opportunities near me." By the time people call their short list of organizations for more information, they know exactly what they are looking for—and that should feel more comfortable than just cold-calling or emailing an organization to inquire in very general terms as to what is going on there that might be a good fit.

Collecting the Rules

As in Mr. Fortenbaugh's case, applying Step 3—collecting lots of knowledge—often means more than just identifying a variety of facts about an opportunity for civic engagement. Rules might come into play too. Consider a decision whether to join an organized group. Maybe someone invites you to a book club. Or you think you need more social interaction but don't know what group to join.

Begin by applying the first two steps of the framework, just as we did with the volunteering question. Step 1 might look identical: What are your goals, and what are the logistical limitations posed by other commitments in your life? Values can be essential here too. You might want to join a church, coach a children's sports team, or join a bird-watching group. Or perhaps you care deeply about adult education, so you want to join a group with like-minded people—like a book club or lecture series on a subject that interests you.

Once you've boiled things down with the first two steps in the framework, you can get online to gather facts under Step 3 about the kinds of groups and organizations that meet the criteria you identified. From there, make some inquiries—calls or emails, if that's more comfortable. And again, maybe ask to speak to a member of the group to get a first-hand feel for the organization and ask very frankly what they wish was different about their experience thus far.

The next part of Step 3 involves identifying rules. In *Hickman v. Taylor*, the rules at issue involved both the possible claims against both the tugboat owners and the B&O Railroad—negligence—and the rules governing the kind of information that the Hickman estate could extract from Fortenbaugh. Rules are crucial to an ordered society and any organization. At work, you might have personnel rules—what the hours of operation are and whether you can take two hours for lunch. If you break the rules, you might lose your job. The same goes for volunteer organizations, of course.

My late father belonged to the Rotary Club in Buffalo, New York. It is an international organization with over 35,000 individual chapters and 1.2 million members. It engages in a range of public service activities, from promoting clean water and fighting disease to fostering education. But to join, you must be invited. The website doesn't make the criteria for membership clear. The criteria for membership are thus something you need to identify before you can make a choice about what group to join. And once you join, there might be rules that govern your conduct. Be sure that you are comfortable with those too. This is all part of gathering knowledge under Step 3 of the B-I-C-A-T framework.

Assessing the Quality of the "Knowledge"

The final piece to Step 3 is assessing the quality of the "knowledge" you've gleaned—both facts and rules—before making your final decision. I put the word "knowledge" in quotes because there is a lot of false and misleading information out there, so it's vital to employ a sorting mechanism to separate good information from bad information. This is basically what happens in court when attorneys make objections to the admission of certain pieces of evidence at trial. There are rules banning certain types of testimony and documents. A judge decides whether a piece of evidence has satisfied the evidentiary rules, which are designed to maximize the legitimacy and authenticity of the information that goes before a jury. If the judge determines that certain information is sketchy, a jury doesn't get to hear it. It's that simple.

There's frankly no reason why, when it comes to decisions of critical importance to our daily lives, we shouldn't be discerning about the kinds of information that goes into our decision-making calculus. The problem is that there isn't a set of rules taped to the fridge that apply to keep bad information from dictating important decisions in our lives. And there isn't a neutral judge on hand to help us separate the unreliable information from the reliable stuff. Step 3 of the framework can assist with that.

For this step, let's focus on two central means of civic engagement: voting and running for office—whether that be U.S. senator or president of the PTA at your child's school. Following the 2020 election, there evolved an excruciating national debate about whether it's worth voting in the first place, given the widespread belief that American elections are unreliable. I'm not going to get into that debate here, except to confess my bias about voting and faith in the work of thousands of Americans—many of whom are volunteers—who make elections function, even in a pandemic. I wrote a whole book on voting called *What You Need to Know About Voting—and Why*, which makes the case for civic engagement at the ballot box regardless of political party. I stand by that position now.

If you are turned off by voting altogether, I urge you to read that book and apply the B-I-C-A-T framework to the question of whether to vote at all. When you get to Step 3, collect information about how the electoral system works in your state and what rules apply to ensure that votes are secure and valid. Once you have that information in hand, and you've broken down your questions about voting (Step 1) and identified your broader values that bear on voting (Step 2), the next task is to figure out what pieces of information are of sufficient quality to guide your decision on whether to vote, and which pieces should be sidelined because their sources are less reliable.

The same framework applies to the question of whom to vote for and even what your position should be on a particular issue, such as climate change regulation or immigration laws. Identify the issue, break it down into sub-parts, identify your values and aim, and then get lots of information. For candidates, you might want to see if their voting records and reputation line up with your values. Say you truly value honesty, for example, and even emphasize that value with your children when they engage in little white lies (as all kids do). You might be a member of the Democratic party but decide to vote for a Republican in a particular election because that person has a reputation for honesty and integrity, and Step 2 of the framework identified those values as paramount to you. Or you might value compromise in relationships, so you vote for a different candidate. You do this not because of adherence to a party or "team," mind you. You do it because you value compromise over party and believe that is how the country moves forward. The values step of the B-I-C-A-T process operates to peer through party lines and black-and-white thinking to help you make the decision based on your own careful assessment of things that matter to you personally.

Candidates aside, the B-I-C-A-T framework can also help you determine where you might come down on issues of national or local importance, like gun control or regulation of the internet. Steps 1 and 2 will help you narrow what matters to you—not just point you to a crowd of social media posters—so you can make a focused, independent decision that you can more easily stand by. On policy issues, it's also vitally helpful to get views on both sides of an issue. This is something that people rarely do, but it can be a game-changer.

In the spring of 2020, I taught a class called "Democracy at Risk" at American University Washington College of Law. There were several hot-button issues on the table that semester, including former President Trump's first impeachment trial, and there were students in the class on both ends of the political spectrum. At the end of the term, I held a Zoom meeting (we were well into the COVID-19 shutdown by then) to take stock of how the semester went. An overwhelming sentiment was that the students surprisingly felt safe talking about difficult issues in class, perhaps for the first time. A significant reason for this could have been that, for each subject matter, I asked students to read two op-eds on the topic before coming to class, and to write a short paragraph on their reactions to the topic thus far.

What happened was two things. First, students came to class

with a deeper understanding of the complexities of an issue than they might have before reading the opinion articles. As I say, life—like law—is rarely black and white. Most critical decisions are complex and fuzzy. National policy debates are no different. Second, students said that their focus in class discussion came from the standpoint of curiosity—not outcomes. They listened to other points of view before forming their own, rather than coming to class with a pre-set team mentality, ready to defend the "party position" on a particular issue.

When you are deciding how to vote or what your take on an issue is, I encourage you to do the same thing—read at least two opinions on a particular issue before making up your mind. When you do read those, scan the opinions for consistency with your own values and aims, which you have identified already under Step 2 of the framework. This is all assuming that the two points of view you have read are based on facts, not lies. (I use that word deliberately, because reliance on lies can be dangerous and we need to be on alert for them.)

So, how do you go about sorting the information that you read online? I get asked this question all the time. Here are a few tips:

- Information that is on an **official government website** is usually reliable because there are established mechanisms of accountability—rules and public scrutiny—that should limit the ability of an official government office to convey blatantly false information to the public.
- Information that links to **original source documents**— such as the actual transcript of a speech or a piece of legislation—is more reliable than a blog that makes

statements with no links or source material. Check out the original sources to confirm that the site is being honest about them.

- Journalists have traditionally abided by the **Society of Professional Journalists' Code of Ethics** that requires things like accuracy, context, use of original sources, and attribution to the work of others. Keep in mind that nobody goes to jail if media coverage doesn't comply with this code—it's like an honor system. But you can bet that traditional media outlets—places like CBS News, ABC News, NBC News, PBS, the *New York Times*, and the *Washington Post*—strive to adhere to these norms. What I tell students is to think of Michael J. Fox in the film *Back to the Future*. If you hop into your DeLorean sports car and go back to the 1980s, what media outlets did people rely on? Those are the same ones that are probably safe bets today.

- If you have never heard of a particular news outlet, **investigate the source before** you believe what you're reading. Sometimes, a quick internet search will reveal it as a propaganda website masquerading as serious journalism. It's also a bad idea to just rely on a Facebook scroll for news because algorithms are feeding you information tailored to what they think you already believe. Pick a few solid journalistic sources and sign up for their newsletters—you'll get a steady stream of news updates every morning.

- As I mentioned earlier, **read opinions on two sides of an issue before making up your mind on your own**

views, and be careful to distinguish opinion from fact-based journalism. Reputable news outlets usually indicate in the section of the paper or website that an article is "opinion" or "commentary." A good op-ed columnist will give hyperlinks or cites to their sources for facts—click on those to confirm what's being said. When you watch cable talk shows, pay attention to when a host turns to a panel for "analysis." This is a discussion of the issues raised by a set of facts that are usually reported by another journalist in the set-up to the discussion. Again, be aware of the distinction between analysis and facts.

The laws governing news do play a role here too. In 1949, the U.S. Federal Communications Commission (FCC)—an independent agency within the federal executive branch—introduced what was known as the "fairness doctrine." The FCC is responsible for licensing television and radio stations. Under the fairness doctrine, to get a license, a station had to agree to present news in a fair, equitable, and balanced manner. Broadcasters had to air controversial information that was of public interest and to give contrasting views. The FCC abolished the policy in 1987. Some people attribute this change as a factor in the rise of unmitigated false information on the internet and certain cable news outlets, which spread it like wildfire.

Also, there's the question of regulating the internet itself. We know from personal experience that broadcast television, cable, and radio have limits on what can be aired—nudity and curse words are forbidden, for example. But the same rules don't apply online, which is why young kids can access pornography inadvertently on their phones. In Section 230 of a statute called the Communications Decency Act of 1996, Congress essentially gave immunity from lawsuits to any online service that publishes the content of third parties. What that means is that any internet service provider (ISP) that posts lies or other disturbing information cannot be held accountable through the legal system. Congress basically decided that sites like YouTube, Yelp, Amazon, Facebook, and Twitter function as bulletin boards in, say, a community recreation center. The recreation center—and certainly the bulletin board itself—isn't responsible for what gets tacked up there.

Suffice it to say that online media giants are a far cry from a community center corkboard. They manage their content in lots of ways that impact people. Politicians from both major political parties have urged Congress to revisit Section 230 and provide more limitations on permissible online content to protect consumers. Stay tuned.

Here's another very important point to keep in mind when it comes to information that comes through your smartphone or computer: Even though we consider our Google searches to be "free," we are actually paying for them—with our personal data. That data is highly valuable, and it's how high-tech companies have made unprecedented amounts of money. With that data, which is bought and sold, retailers apply algorithms to push information into our news and social media feeds. In the 1980s, everyone got the same set of news on the pages of a newspaper or magazine. Today, what I get is different from what you get—and that depends on the algorithm "reading" your data to feed you information that is valuable to big corporations. In a more ideal world, we can imagine this paradigm shifting—where big companies must pay us to use the information gleaned from clicks and swipes. Imagine how that would change things. Regular people could make money by allowing companies to use their data—otherwise it stays confidential—rather than the other way around. But that would require legislators to step up to the plate and do something.

This is all by way of saying that—unlike keeping airplanes safe when we board them or plowing roads during a snowstorm—government is not taking meaningful steps to prevent regular people from getting rivers of garbage information into their brains that are targeted from big corporations and even foreign governments. Perhaps worse, our data can be used not only by retailers who want to make money off us, but by governments that might want to track us. Although there's not much that can be done by users about big data surveillance, we can and should learn to self-police the data that comes through our personal technology and into our brains, because it has an impact on our families and future generations. In my view, this is one of the biggest challenges of the twenty-first century—one that was unfathomable just a couple of decades ago.

Okay, so we've worked through the nuances of Step 3. Let's apply it to a civic engagement problem: running for office. This can be at the local, state, or federal level—or it could be for a homeowners' association, PTA president (some are elected), glee club director, or union leadership. The positions may or may not be paid but are often part-time. They can be topic specific—like a school board member or election official—or more general, like a state or federal legislator, a mayor or city council member, a district attorney or sheriff, or even a judge (except at the federal level, where judges are appointed by the president and confirmed by the U.S. Senate under the Constitution).

Step 1 is to break the problem down. Here's a crack at an initial list of sub-issues that you might consider:

- Whether to run
- What office to run for
- Raising money, staff, and volunteers (if needed)

From here, you can identify sub-categories within each category, like the following:

- Whether to run
    - Who else is running
    - Competing life/professional issues
        - Finances
        - Other employment conflicts
        - Children at home
- What office to run for
    - Any volunteer or prior experience bearing on this question
    - Values and aims (see Step 2)
    - Competing life/professional issues
- Raising money, staff, and volunteers
    - Feedback from friends and colleagues
    - Availability of support from other organizations or people
    - Budget

This list is hardly exhaustive—you can see how it could get much more detailed and expansive. Once you do Step 2, values and aims, you might be better positioned to come back and answer whether to run and if so, what office to run for—and when. It's especially important that you identify why you are running so that you can share that message with people who have influence in the organization you are seeking to lead. It will also keep you going in the moments where you otherwise might quit because of the challenges of the process.

For this decision, Step 3 will entail more rules than many other life decisions. Each organization has its rules governing eligibility to get on the ballot—age, nationality, residence, etc.—and filing deadlines and fees, especially if it's for political office. You need to find those out. You will want to produce a time line for getting things done—which could also derive from legal requirements—as well as create a database of donors and volunteers (if necessary) and an analysis of how to get them on board.

After this quick drive-through application of the B-I-C-A-T framework to a decision to run for some sort of office, it's evident that the process is often not for the faint of heart. But hopefully, framing it around the five steps of legal analysis makes it seem surmountable. Leadership at all levels of community is a crucial part of American democracy and one that more regular people—friends and neighbors like you and me—should be able to access readily. If that were the case, our government could look very different—much more like the general population.

STEP 3 CHECKLIST: COLLECTING KNOWLEDGE

✓ What is the decision you are making?

✓ What are the possible sources of information bearing on this issue? (Think about what search terms to use in an internet search. Did you capture a range of views?)

✓ Assess the quality and legitimacy of each of the sources you are considering.

✓ Is it a government-run site?

✓ If not, is it a *Back to the Future*–type source (one that existed in the 1980s when serious journalism was easier to identify)?

✓ If you have never heard of the source, do a separate search to identify whether the source is known for bias one way or another.

✓ What original sources are available on the issue (e.g., actual scientific studies, memoranda with the writer's signature, or transcripts of a speech—rather than someone else's summary)?

✓ List all the information that you gathered. Circle the critical pieces.

✓ List all the rules or standards that might govern your decision.

4

Thinking Like a Lawyer in Health Care Decisions

> Divide each difficulty into as many parts as is feasible and necessary to resolve it, and watch the whole transform.
> —RENÉ DESCARTES

When it comes to things that Americans *really* care about, health care is a huge priority. In April 2020, a survey by the Kaiser Family Foundation showed that a substantial majority of all voters—or 63%—ranked health care as an issue of top concern for the November election. Health care was more important than national security, taxes, immigration, and climate change. Only the subject of the economy (which includes jobs) came close, in second place. On the topic of health care, respondents identified increased access to medical care as the biggest issue, followed by the high cost of health care and health insurance. A substantial 69% of those surveyed favored access to some form of a government-administered health care plan for everyone, rather than relying on private insurance companies plus Medicare (for the elderly) and Medicaid (for low-income families).

Americans' deep focus on health care is, of course, perfectly understandable. Personal health is a matter of life and death itself. In 2019, there were 2,854,838 deaths in the United States, and an infant mortality rate of 5.58 deaths per 1,000 live births. Although the average life expectancy in the United States is high these days by comparison to the history of humankind—78.8 years (a figure that dipped a full year after the COVID-19 pandemic)—many deaths would be preventable with better access to health care. Heart disease is the leading cause of death, claiming 659,041 Americans in 2019, followed by cancer, which took 599,601 lives. Chronic lower respiratory disease caused by factors such as tobacco smoking (including second-hand smoke), air pollution, and allergens claimed 156,979 lives. Another 150,005 died of stroke and 121,499 of Alzheimer's disease. Just under 50,000 people died of influenza and pneumonia combined in the United States in 2019—approximately the same number that died by suicide. Unintentional injuries or accidents led to 173,040 deaths, a relatively small percentage by comparison to the many health-related causes.

Readers no doubt have heard and maybe even employed the old adage, "If you have your health, you have everything." And if you've been through a health scare personally or lost a close friend or family member to illness, you know that there's a certain clarity that one's diminished health brings to the complexities of life. Things that once bothered you now seem trivial. So, it stands to reason that health care decisions are indisputably some of the most important decisions we make in life. They can produce both miraculous and devastating consequences.

Should you get elective surgery to aid crushing back pain if there's a chance it could make things worse? What about liposuction to address self-esteem issues, which are not life-threatening but debilitating? Should you go on a medication to lower your cholesterol, or anti-depressants to help with anxiety, despite the side effects and even social stigma? How about childbirth—should you opt for having your baby in the hospital or at home, and should it be with or without pain medication?

When you're looking for a doctor or trying to decide whether to take a particular doctor's advice, how do you decide whether to trust that person with your health—and even your life? If you or a loved one winds up in the hospital, how do you manage care from the sidelines? Should you second-guess your doctors or stay out of the way—and if you do get deliberately involved, on which questions is it worth stepping in forcefully? Studies show that more than 8% of individuals aged eighteen and over don't get needed medical care due to cost. How do you juggle the price tag of health care with other pressing priorities in your life?

Importantly, when it comes to health care, there are also some basic legal documents that need to be in order. For anyone aged eighteen or older—including adult children—it's extremely helpful to execute a document that identifies a person you trust who can make decisions about your health care if you are incapacitated. This is known as a "health care proxy" or "health care power of attorney"—but it's not the same thing as a power of attorney for legal and financial decisions if you cannot make them for yourself. You need in your file cabinet *both* a legal power of attorney *and* a health care proxy to cover all the bases.

Among your health care documents, you can choose in advance what kind of medical treatments you want in the event of a serious accident or other catastrophe, including whether you want to be resuscitated if your heart stops. Only about a third of Americans have something like this on hand, which people also call a "living will." This statistic means that two-thirds of Americans could one day wind up at the mercy of a judgment about their life or death that they possibly wouldn't agree with if they were well enough to make the decision themselves. Not having a health care proxy on hand can also be extremely stressful and divisive for family members who might disagree on the best course of treatment for you, with no guidance from the person whose life may be at stake.

Using the basic skills of thinking like a lawyer can come in handy in the health care arena, especially because health care decisions often trigger strong emotions and impact a range of people you care about. Under worst-case scenarios, health care gone wrong can lead to death or serious disabilities, as well as the possibility of painful litigation against a hospital or doctors. We will talk about when it might be time to hire a lawyer across a range of issues in Chapter 5.

For now, let's return to the five-part B-I-C-A-T framework for legal decision-making that we have been breaking down throughout this book:

1. **Break** the problem down.
2. **Identify** your values and your aim.

3. **Collect** lots of knowledge.
4. **Argue** both sides of each point.
5. **Tolerate** the fact that people will disagree with your choice—and that you might feel conflicted.

In this chapter, we will focus on **Step 4: Argue both sides of each point.** We were introduced to this vital concept in Chapter 3 when talking about collecting lots of knowledge—both in terms of relevant facts and in terms of relevant rules of the game—before making a decision of some consequence. Step 4 addresses what you do with all of the knowledge once it's out on the table.

Recall too that we talked earlier about the phenomenon of confirmation bias—the natural human tendency to look for or interpret evidence in a way that confirms a pre-existing belief rather than approaching new information from a neutral and curious point of view. Imagine that you and your partner together decide to get a pet. You have your heart set on a dog, but your partner grew up with cats. Perhaps you do an internet search of the question, "Are dogs better pets than cats?" The search query itself shows a bias that will probably sort the search results for pro-dog articles. But even if you entered a more neutral question like, "Which is the best house pet?" confirmation bias might render you more inclined to focus on any information that comes up praising the attributes of dogs, rather than considering the benefits of getting a cat with an equally open mind.

Likewise, if (like my late father) you simply "hate hospitals," you may dismiss the benefits of elective surgery out-of-hand and singularly focus on the downsides of a hospital admission, recovery process, and the side effects of a procedure that might even save your life when a more balanced approach would be better for your health overall.

Lawyers know to sort for the potholes in their client's case as diligently as they gather arguments in favor of a client's preferred outcome. But this skill is not inherent. The law school curriculum often breaks legal writing instruction into two separate courses—one that teaches the skill of writing a memorandum that makes a recommendation to a client, and a second that teaches the skill of writing a piece of actual advocacy urging one outcome over another. This is an important bifurcation because, after years of watching actors pose as lawyers in television trial dramas, students often expect that the role of a lawyer is to argue vigorously for a client no matter what. But persuading a judge or decision-maker of a particular point of view is only one of the skills of a lawyer. In England, it's only a special kind of lawyer— known as a "barrister"—that gets to do that in a courtroom. Another kind of lawyer—a "solicitor"—prepares the underlying legal documentation.

For American lawyers, it's important to have both skills. Sometimes a client will come to a lawyer wanting to file a lawsuit. If the lawyer does some research and finds out that the client's complaint is not one that the legal system will likely address, it's the lawyer's job to explain that problem to the client.

Here's a common-sense example of how a lawyer might need to deliver bad news to a client, because the law says so.

In class, I often give a hypothetical about someone getting "stink-eye" from a lady on the subway. The angry gaze really upsets the plaintiff, who wants to hire a lawyer to sue the lady for the emotional pain and suffering the plaintiff's experience of the stink-eye caused her. Maybe the lady triggered something very traumatic in the plaintiff's past, making her claim of emotional damage all too real. There is no legal cause of action—no right to go to court and get money—for stink-eye, however. A legislature could decide to create such a claim, but for now, the courts are not the pathway to a remedy for stink-eye. A lawyer would be obliged to tell the client as much.

Now, it's conceivable that there does exist a law that could possibly be stretched to cover stink-eye. In the stink-eye hypothetical, a lawyer might try to stretch laws that ban what's called "intentional infliction of emotional distress" to cover stink-eye, but before filing that claim, they would have to consider the downsides. Because there's no such law on the books, the client would likely lose the case—and the attorneys' fees spent on attempting to litigate it. The lawyer and the client would also potentially be subject to monetary sanctions from a court if the claim is considered frivolous to the extreme.

With any litigation, moreover, there are the downsides of delays, anxiety, and stress, and the impossibility of predicting how a jury or court will rule even under a set of facts and legal framework that seem to be very favorable to the client. In a memorandum, the lawyer might lay the pros and cons out before ultimately making a recommendation.

If the client decides to move forward with the stink-eye case, that's where the art of advocacy would come into play. The lawyer would pick a side and argue to the court that it is the legally correct side. The lawyer might head the other side's counterarguments off in footnotes, knowing that the judge will likely hear them at some point. But the aim of the argument is not to neutrally and evenly assess the situation, but instead to bring the court around to seeing a very specific point of view.

Now consider this: Which approach to decision-making would you prefer to bring to an important health care decision—assessment or advocacy? The answer should be obvious: You want to read the "pros and cons" memo, not the one that decidedly presses a particular outcome, if the question is one that could affect your health, and possibly even teeter on questions of life and death. But with confirmation bias already working against you inadvertently, training yourself to walk through a decision more methodically by using the lawyering skills set forth in this book could be worth the extra time.

A Law School Lesson: *Evening Star Newspaper Company v. Kemp*

How Do Lawyers Prepare to Argue Both Sides of an Issue?

Time now for another law school lesson to underscore the importance of arguing both sides of an issue—because again, most decisions in law, like in life, involve lots of gray areas. Few are black and white. But to see the shades of gray, you have to widen the aperture of your lens in the first place.

Evening Star Newspaper Company v. Kemp involved a truck driver named Nathan Kemp who delivered papers for a newspaper called the *Evening Star*. He owned his own taxicab on the side, which he operated part-time. One August day in 1971, Kemp returned from a newspaper delivery run to the Evening Star facility at around 3:30 p.m. He was due to make another run at 4:25 p.m. but was still on pay status—or "on the clock"—while he waited during that interim hour. Another employee told Kemp that his cab, which was parked a half-block away, had been hit by another vehicle. Kemp and two other employees—the guy who told him about the accident, who was named Andrews, and another who did body work on cars named Ward—left the Evening Star building to check out the cab. Andrews saw the dent in the cab and told Kemp that if he had a rubber mallet, he could fix it well enough to get the cab through an inspection.

The three returned to the Evening Star garage with the cab and found a mallet. While Andrews was working on the dent, Ward grabbed a gun that Kemp kept in the trunk of his cab as a safety measure in case he was robbed or assaulted while driving the cab. Ward began handling the gun, and it went off accidentally, killing Kemp. Ward testified: "And like I had the gun in my hand, and he said, 'Oh, man, come on, let's stop this playing.' And he made a motion towards me and hit my hand and the gun went off."

Kemp's widow sought compensation from the Evening Star under a statute called the Longshoreman's and Harbor Workers' Compensation Act. Under the statute, if Kemp's death arose out of his employment or in the course of his employment, she could get paid workers' compensation benefits. If her husband's death did not arise out of his employment, the widow could get nothing from the Evening Star.

Now, you can imagine what the widow's lawyer argued: that the lag time between Kemp's 3:30 p.m. and 4:25 p.m. runs was still on the clock, so the death arose out of his job. The company let the drivers do whatever they wanted during this downtime, and in the past others had borrowed tools from the garage to work on their personal vehicles. The drivers' supervisors knew all of this and allowed it to happen. The widow's lawyer also argued that Kemp kept the gun because he was afraid of being mugged while he delivered papers, particularly because his truck looked a lot like the trucks used by the company to carry money. The widow testified that she was with him a few times when he carried the gun to pick up his paycheck at the Evening Star, so the gun was tangentially part of the job. Moreover, several other employees had been threatened on their delivery runs and carried guns in their personal cars.

This all sounds perfectly reasonable and maybe even correct, right? If you were the lawyer for the widow, confirmation bias might lure you into gathering every possible factoid in defense of your client's claim that Kemp was on the clock when he was killed, and that the Evening Star had to pay his widow workers' compensation benefits. Why not just stop there? Why, in other words, is it important for the lawyer to excavate and rehearse the other side of the case too—even before making the arguments for Kemp's widow?

For starters, the judge is going to want to hear both sides. Judges—unlike politicians—are required to weigh the evidence and the law fairly and impartially to the extent humanly possible. This is because the rules of evidence and other procedural rules require it. That's a good thing, because it fosters fairness and even-handedness across the board.

But don't be fooled—judges have lots of discretion, nonetheless. (Anyone who tells you that "good" judges apply the plain language of the law without interpreting anything or using their own discretion to resolve ambiguities is selling something—it's just not true.) In this case, the discretion revolved around the meaning of the statute's words that the injury or death "arose in the course of employment." Obvious, you say? He died in connection with his job.

Not so fast.

Evening Star's lawyers argued that, sure, the three employees were on an authorized break when Kemp was killed. But Kemp severed or broke away from his employment when he and his buddies started playing around with a personal handgun. Had the injury been sustained in a brawl using a wrench lying around in the employer's garage, then the employer would more obviously be liable. But it can't be said that the fatal shooting "arose out of" his employment—Kemp wasn't doing anything on behalf of the Evening Star when he was killed. The newspaper didn't issue its employees guns, and probably for good reason: they can be deadly in the hands of untrained people. If Kemp had a gun and nobody at the company did anything about it, that doesn't mean it somehow justifies compensation to the widow.

It turns out that the wife's arguments carried the day in *Evening Star Newspaper Company v. Kemp*. The court ruled in her favor, writing: "We are aware of the fact . . . that decedent had already taken one run in a truck without a pistol, but this did not negate the possibility that another assigned run, after a waiting period, might involve a function (being given money to turn in), time, or route that would lead him to carry a gun in the truck. The gun did not provide an automatic severance from employment."

Note that the court's ruling rebutted the arguments that Evening Star would have likely made against authorizing money for the widow. In other words, it responded to the critiques of the widow's arguments, which presumably came from Evening Star's lawyers. To win their case, then, the widow's lawyers *had* to anticipate the arguments against her and head them off in their briefs. Simply listing all the reasons she should win, even strenuously—without explaining why the arguments against her should also be rejected—might have produced a different outcome for the widow.

Consider next a "stretching" hypothetical, using *Evening Star Newspaper Company v. Kemp.* Imagine that the government employs a park ranger named Lund to protect and patrol certain forest areas against illegal hunting. Lund has the night shift, and the government gives him a vehicle with a seat that can be converted into a bed so he can rest while in the woods. One morning, after an overnight patrol, Lund is found dead in the vehicle with a dead woman next to him. Her personal car is parked alongside his government-owned vehicle. The two bodies are topless and partially covered by a blanket. The ranger's boots and uniform are under the front seat.

It turns out the deaths were caused by carbon monoxide poisoning and the time of death was somewhere between 1 a.m. and 3 p.m. The government-owned car was in an area that has been under surveillance for illegal deer hunting, and there is no employment rule against having visitors while on duty.

Lund's widow sues under the same statute that was at issue in *Evening Star.* The question again is whether her husband's death arose out of the scope of his employment and whether, unlike in *Evening Star*, Lund's apparent carrying on an extra-marital affair severed his employment during the hours that it took place.

If you represent Lund's widow, what arguments would you make? To begin with, you would argue that the case is just like *Evening Star*—there was no rule against doing personal things while on breaks. This is the "me too!" argument I've mentioned before. In *Evening Star*, Kemp was fixing his cab, which had nothing to do with his paper route. In Lund's case, he was sleeping, which was completely *within* the scope of his job description, so it's even a better case for compensation than *Evening Star,* and the widow in that case did get paid. Why give him a car with a bed in it if it's not expected that he would sleep in it? By the same token, Lund was in the area where deer had been killed so it is evident that he was working at the time, even while sleeping. Having a visitor was not off limits, and his activity with her had nothing to do with his ability to do his job; whether it affected his marriage was beside the point.

Again, this argument sounds fairly good, but what about counter-arguments? The government would argue that he didn't have his uniform on—or even a shirt—so he was hardly in a position to kick into gear and provide surveillance at a moment's notice, which is what he was being paid for. Having secret sex while on duty is not part of the job, at least for park rangers. The facts of *Evening Star* were different because the gun was something that could be used to secure the vehicle while carrying money for the newspaper. There's zero benefit to the employer in Lund's having extra-marital affairs while on the job. If he wants to do that, so be it—but on his own time. He should be considered "off the clock" during the hours of 1 a.m. and 3 a.m. that night, at least.

Now ask yourself: Did this discussion surprise you in any way? Any lightbulbs go off about arguing both sides? Hopefully, the answer is yes.

When I was a first-year law student at the University of Michigan, we were given one "side" of a case to represent in a legal writing exercise. I was convinced my client was correct on all fronts and wrote the briefs accordingly. (In fact, I won an award for the strongest written advocacy in that class that year.) Once it came time to deliver oral argument on the briefs we wrote, the instructor did a switcheroo: We were to argue the *other* side's case—not the side that we argued in our carefully written work. It was *the* lightbulb moment for me in law school, because once I dug into the other side, I found myself convinced that it had the better argument, not the side I had originally represented in my brief. The lesson, of course, was that there are two sides to every coin when it comes to most litigation and many routine legal issues. A good lawyer identifies both.

In everyday life, we are not as incentivized to see both sides of an issue with an open mind. There is no judge that needs convincing when it comes to decisions that affect our lives, so there's little need to identify rebuttals of the arguments against our opening position. The only "judge" is the happenstance of our life trajectories (i.e., how things turn out in the short and long runs). Or maybe we have a spouse or family member that has a stake in things and a different point of view. Either way, training ourselves to identify both sides of an issue in a methodical way—just like lawyers do—can be helpful in maximizing the chance of a really good decision.

Now back to the B-I-C-A-T framework, and Step 4: Argue both sides of each point.

Argue Both Sides

Let's consider the question of whether to have elective surgery. Your vision has declined, and an ophthalmologist tells you that the reason is cataracts, which means that you have clouded lenses in your eyes. Lenses are usually transparent. Surgery can be performed to remove the cloudy lenses and replace them with artificial ones. The condition is not life-threatening, but surgery could increase the quality of your life substantially.

Recall where we are in the framework so far: You will have broken down the problem, identified your values and your aim, and collected lots of information. **Step 1** might look like this:

- Medical risks
    - Side effects
    - Recovery period
    - Choosing a provider
- Benefits of clear vision
    - Work requirements
    - Logistics of life (driving, reading, watching TV, etc.)

- Costs
    - Insurance coverage
    - Out-of-pocket
    - Other competing financial obligations

Step 2, identifying your values and your aim, could mean different things depending on the elective surgery at issue. Eye surgery could lead to better vision and quality of life. By contrast, a procedure like breast augmentation might mean enhancement of self-esteem, or perhaps enhanced work opportunities for women in the entertainment industry. During the COVID-19 pandemic, with medical staff stretched thin, identifying public health as a personal value could also tip the decision to get elective surgery into the future—after the vaccination program took hold sufficiently to give hospitals some breathing room, and variants of the coronavirus have subsided.

Step 3, collecting lots of knowledge, would require learning about the details of cataract surgery, which entails cutting out an existing lens or breaking it up into little pieces and then removing the pieces and replacing the lens with an artificial one made of plastic, acrylic, or silicone. There is a 90% success rate, but risks include inflammation, infection, bleeding, swelling, droopy lids, glaucoma, and even loss of vision. It's generally done on an outpatient basis by an ophthalmologist.

Finding out which kinds of medical accreditations are optimal for doctors who perform this surgery—an ophthalmologist went to medical school, for example, while an optometrist did not—is another important component of information-gathering. Yet consider the fact that dentists have been known to perform plastic surgery. One dentist reportedly did a breast reduction on a fifteen-year-old patient, leaving her disfigured. You want the right doctor for the job. So, it's vital that you collect information about best practices for the kind of procedure you are considering and get a second opinion on the recommendation to have the surgery. Then do research on the specific doctor or practice you are contemplating—just because a friend recommends a particular doctor doesn't mean that doctor is right for you and your procedure. And check in advance with your insurance company to find out how much of it will be covered.

Now for **Step 4**. Imagine that you are fairly confident that you want to go ahead with the surgery. In other words, your bias goes in that direction. List all the reasons why it's a good idea. The list might look something like this:

- It could clear up your vision enough to drive and watch TV, which have been a problem for you.
- The procedure is covered by insurance with a small deductible.
- Side effects are rare.

Then list the counter-arguments for each. This is the step that counteracts confirmation bias that is a natural—but not necessarily comprehensive—means of making decisions.

- It's possible that it won't help, which would mean a lot of hassle for nothing.
- It's covered by insurance, but recovery can take up to three months, during which you might have problems

at work that might require you taking time off; that risk complicates the financial benefits of doing the surgery.
- Although rare, side effects do happen, and can be devastating—like total loss of vision.

Finally, just as the lawyers for the Kemp widow likely did in the *Evening Star* case, list the rebuttals to each counter-argument:

- The success rate is 90% and the side effects are relatively minor. If this were major back surgery, which can leave people incapacitated for weeks, this factor might weigh more heavily towards caution. But not here.
- Your boss is fairly understanding, and many people began telecommuting during the COVID-19 pandemic anyway, so this might in fact be an opportune time to have the surgery.
- If you were considering whether to get Lasik surgery to avoid wearing glasses, the risk of a serious problem might outweigh the benefits, particularly if you are over forty and will probably need reading lenses anyway. But the cataracts are affecting your ability to see even with glasses, so the tiny chance that things will go wrong is outweighed by the upsides. You also have done a deep dive into your doctor's success rate and reputation, and you feel confident that you are going to be in very experienced hands. Here again, things might be different if the only doctor available was fresh out of medical training and hadn't done many of these surgeries yet.

The framework can be applied to any health care decision you need to make—including decisions you face while you or a loved one is in the hospital. Often you have to make calls quickly in a hospital setting, when doctors only do their "rounds" once a day and might catch you off guard and unprepared for a serious conversation—if at all. Just because you are admitted to a hospital doesn't mean that you will be taken care of in terms of having good decisions made. No one else is probably doing anything like a thorough B-I-C-A-T analysis for each medical decision for you, many of which can have significant consequences. Keeping a decision checklist by your bedside or giving the framework to a loved one who is helping you through the process can pay dividends in the long run.

Again, one thing to keep in mind is that it's always a good idea, if possible, to sit with a decision after you have gotten through Step 4. Give it twenty-four hours or even twenty minutes, if possible. Research shows that our brains continue to subconsciously process information while our cognitive attention turns to something else. In other words, your brain can walk and chew gum at the same time. Take advantage of that fact and trust yourself—and your brain—with it.

Health Law Basics

Let's next walk through some of the legal basics that impact health care. Law school courses in health law teach students about private health insurance and how it's regulated by state and federal law, as well as the two existing public health insurance options: Medicare and Medicaid. The Affordable Care Act, also known as Obamacare or the ACA, is a law that expanded eligibility for Medicaid in 2010 and made changes to the market for individual insurance. Perhaps most significantly, insurers were required to accept all applicants regardless of pre-existing health conditions.

There are many other laws that implicate health care, including laws banning health care providers from committing fraud against private insurance companies and the Medicare and Medicaid programs, such as by falsely billing for reimbursement of health care services that were not provided. There are also various laws governing the licensing of health care professionals and accreditation of facilities like nursing homes. Finally, there are privacy and security laws that you encounter when you're asked to sign several forms when you go to the doctor. The primary one is called the Health Insurance Portability and Accountability Act of 1996, or HIPAA, and it gives you rights to control your health information and sets rules on who can look at it, among other matters. Of course, enforcement of these laws is a critical mechanism for minimizing corruption and incompetence in the health care system.

The B-I-C-A-T framework could help narrow options in your search for a health care plan, especially if there are a lot of confusing options available. Breaking up the decision into pieces, identifying values and goals, and gathering information about each piece of the decision can go a long way toward bringing some order to the chaos. There are dozens of online websites where you can access do-it-yourself legal services for basic things like living wills, health care proxies, and advance care directives—the documents that give someone you trust control over your health care in case you are incapacitated. The biggest name is probably LegalZoom, but sites like Rocket Lawyer and IncFile (for business formation) also have standard "boilerplate" forms. Because the laws vary by state, it's important that you get the right requirements for where you live. But getting these documents in order is worth the effort and marginal cost—for your sake, and for the sake of your family.

STEP 4 CHECKLIST: ARGUE BOTH SIDES

✓ What is the decision facing you?

✓ Identify what your likely "bias" is—how do you feel inclined to come out on an issue in your "gut"?

✓ List all the reasons why the outcome you likely favor is the correct one. (If you don't have any idea, just pick a side.)

✓ For every argument you listed in favor of one side, list a counter-argument—even if you don't think it's particularly persuasive. Just list something.

✓ Identify rebuttals to your counter-arguments next—that is, why is the first "side" the better one after all?

✓ Set the lists aside for a day, or even a few hours, before assessing the strengths and weaknesses of your initial bias.

5

Thinking Like a Lawyer in Hiring a Lawyer

> To me, a lawyer is basically the person that knows the rules of the country. We're all throwing the dice, playing the game, moving our pieces around the board, but if there is a problem, the lawyer is the only person who has read the inside of the top of the box.
> —JERRY SEINFELD

No matter how well you may have learned to think like a lawyer, there may also come a time when you simply can't "do it yourself" and need to hire someone with a degree. Should that happen, there are several things to keep in mind. One is that not all lawyers can help with all legal questions. Like doctors, lawyers tend to specialize in certain kinds of laws. Family lawyers know about divorce. Trust and estate lawyers can draft wills. Bankruptcy lawyers help clients reorganize if they can't pay their bills. Tax lawyers know a lot about the complexities of the federal and state tax codes. And so on.

Lawyers don't just differ in their areas of subject matter

expertise, but also in their skill sets. Compared to tax codes, criminal laws are not especially complicated. They largely entail a list of elements of a crime that prosecutors must prove beyond a reasonable doubt, and possible defenses that the lawyer for the defendant can raise to prevent a conviction. Criminal law thus turns a lot on the facts. Accordingly, criminal lawyers are often particularly skilled at uncovering facts through witnesses and documents and connecting the dots. Constitutional law, by contrast, is laden with policy and theory. Lawyers with expertise on this subject must be steeped in the rationales behind certain constitutional provisions and how the law has developed over the years in the Supreme Court. They might focus less on building a narrative through facts. Lawyers who practice as mediators are skilled at negotiation—identifying the heart of a controversy and the various stakeholders' fears and goals and attempting to move toward a resolution by pointing out incentives for compromise. And so on.

Within a particular area of expertise, moreover, lawyers have varying styles and approaches. I tell my students to be mindful of their professional reputations when out in the real world. If you are known as someone who is reasonable and can be worked with, you will more readily gain the trust of an opposing party's counsel and even judges. Some lawyers are known for playing hardball and even skirting ethical boundaries. That kind of lawyer can be highly effective, depending on the case and the issues at stake for the client, but it comes at a cost. Often, people hire well-known lawyers due to their stellar reputations, not realizing that what they're probably getting is engagement of that lawyer's lower-level associates. Lawyers who spend their time "making rain"—or getting clients—might not be the ones actually doing the work. When hiring a lawyer, it's helpful to be aware of these various distinctions so you can choose the kind of lawyer that fits your needs.

I learned about the more nuanced distinctions between lawyers when I found myself needing to hire one during a painful and contentious divorce. The thought of hiring a lawyer was terrifying and even appalling to me, as it signaled escalation, expense, and tension. But when I received an email from my ex-husband's recently hired lawyer, I knew I had to do something quickly. I chose a person whose reputation was framed around mediation, in the hopes that we could resolve things efficiently and amicably. But my ex hired someone with a reputation for being highly aggressive—freezing bank accounts, filing lawsuits for custody, and the like, presumably on the strategy that the pressure would force an advantageous settlement for the client.

After our first mediation session, we had loosely agreed on the major elements of a settlement around property and custody. But before we could finish hammering out the details, the mediator announced at 6 p.m. on a Friday that she had to leave and ended the session. Over the weekend, my ex's lawyer convinced him to back out of the entire deal, returning us to square one in the standoff. I knew I needed to find a tougher lawyer for myself. And I located one. Once I hired him, we had a settlement within a few weeks—but only after I spent a treacherous eight months and thousands of dollars wasted on the wrong lawyer.

This chapter is about more than just how to hire a lawyer. It's about the final step in the B-I-C-A-T framework: Tolerate the fact that people will disagree with your choice—and that you might feel conflicted. For several reasons, this is perhaps the most important step in the framework, and one that I learned personally through my divorce experiences. Recall the discussion in Chapter 2 around family law, and the widely shared expectation that, if a case goes to trial, many judges will simply divide up custody and things 50/50. Knowing that is likely the case, divorcing couples may be told by friends and those familiar with the process to simply sit down with their spouse and hammer out a 50/50 deal, thus saving tens of thousands of dollars in legal fees—not to mention the stress associated with a drawn-out process.

My ex and I received that very advice, but emotions ran high, and vindicating a side and "winning" arguably eclipsed reason for a time, including on the subject of what was likely best for the kids. After our first mediation failed, I realized I had to prioritize getting through the process over scoring points. We settled the second time we tried mediation. The alternative would have likely been a trial, and lots of legal fees, and possibly a judge deciding things in a way I didn't like anyway. But to move on swiftly, and reap the benefits that come with that, I had to give some things up. The last step of the framework helps explain why.

Let's return for the final time to the five-part B-I-C-A-T framework:

1. **Break** the problem down.
2. **Identify** your values and your aim.
3. **Collect** lots of knowledge.
4. **Argue** both sides of each point.
5. **Tolerate** the fact that people will disagree with your choice—and that you might feel conflicted.

In this chapter, we will focus on **Step 5: Tolerate the fact that people will disagree with your choice—and that you might feel conflicted.** This step touches on something that lawyers understand and tell their clients every day: There is no guarantee that you will win a case, or even get everything you are looking for. You could lose the case completely. And if you go into settlement discussions, especially through a mediator, you will wind up having to give things up that might be really important to you—or to someone else who cares about the process.

Lawyers can have the best case under the sun and not convince a judge. Judges can be unpredictable, even with what appear to be strong laws and strong facts. And sometimes, litigation is unavoidable. Imagine that a party breaches a contract by refusing to pay for the work you did renovating a kitchen and won't return your phone calls. You invested a lot in the job and cannot reasonably walk away without being paid. So, you sue. You know you might lose, but you decide that you have to at least try to get your money.

Sometimes, it makes more sense to walk away from a dispute, even if that choice feels unfair. But moving on can be a win, actually. If you think about your values and your goals, and the arguments for and against both sides of the relevant issues, cutting your losses can be the strongest option. For me in my divorce, moving on was more important than "winning." Achieving a "better" outcome would have come at a price if I were able to achieve it at all. I decided that "losing" some things was winning, at least according to my own value system in that moment.

Typically, an alternative to Step 5 of the framework is black-and-white thinking, or what psychologists call "splitting." In its worse form, splitting can be a symptom of borderline personality disorder, a serious psychiatric condition. But in everyday life, separating "good" from "bad" and "right" from "wrong" with no in-between is fairly common. It's efficient and comfortable, but often ignores the inevitable gray areas of life and the richness that comes with nuance.

When it comes to decision-making, black-and-white thinking can get you really stuck. It can strain your relationships as a result, depriving you of the grace that comes with acceptance. Black-and-white thinking can also make you especially hard on yourself if you apply to yourself the same harsh filter that you apply to others. And in the workplace, it can prompt you to avoid failure, which in turn can deprive you of successes—because, as Henry Ford said, "Failure is simply the opportunity to begin again, this time more intelligently." Studies show that binary thinking also tends to just make you feel bad.

In law, refusing to accept gray areas or the reality of a loss can get lawyers—and clients—in real trouble. A case I teach my first years shows how.

A Law School Lesson: *Patsy's Brand, Inc. v. I.O.B. Realty, Inc.*

How and Why Must Lawyers and Their Clients Learn to Accept Losses?

Patsy's Brand, Inc. v. I.O.B. Realty, Inc. is a case about trademark law, but I use it with my law students to talk about the role of lawyers in lawsuits, and why they can't ignore bad facts and bad law. They must accept the reality of a case if it has weaknesses and share the bad news with their clients. Black-and-white thinking is risky for lawyers.

Bear in mind that trademark law protects a particular party's right to exclusively identify goods by a word, phrase, symbol, or logo. Think golden arches for McDonald's or the bite-out-of-the-apple symbol for Apple Inc. In 1994, a company called Patsy's Brand, Inc. began selling jarred spaghetti sauce with labels bearing the name "Patsy's." It later sued a company with the clunky name "Patsy's Pizzeria, I.O.B. Realty, Inc.," claiming that the pizzeria was selling sauce with the name Patsy's, in violation of trademark law and Patsy's trademarked label. The pizzeria hired a law firm to defend it against Patsy's motion for a preliminary injunction—that is, a request that the court immediately order the pizzeria to stop using labels with the name "Patsy's."

The law firm submitted to the court a sworn affidavit—or written statement—by Frank Brija, an owner of the pizzeria, stating that: "The labels display an exact copy of PATSY'S® old menu covers and other features of our restaurant that we have been using for over six decades. The labels display an exact copy of PATSY'S® restaurant's logo, colors and artwork that we have been using since we opened in 1933." The affidavit went on to claim that Brija had hired a firm called Keller Label & Ticket Company to print the labels, "and asked them to make the label in a dark green color since this was the color PATSY'S® is famous for using, an institutional dark green color." Brija stated that his restaurant has "been selling sauce in a mason jar with the label at issue since at least the spring of 1993," and produced invoices from Keller Label & Ticket Company dating back to 1993.

In response, Patsy's lawyer pointed out that Brija's label contained a bar code that didn't even exist until 1998, so it could not have been used since 1993. Moreover, the invoices listed an area code that did not exist until after 1993.

Brija had lied. His lawyers quit the case.

Later, the court granted Patsy's motion for a preliminary injunction, ordering the pizzeria to stop using the labels but keeping the case open so the parties could produce further evidence on the question of whether the trademark was violated.

So, take note of where things stand: client lied, lawyer submitted the lies to the court, lawyer quit when it became apparent what happened, court ruled for the other side. The liar lost.

Brija wasn't willing to give up. He was mired in black-and-white thinking, that is, he was insistent that he should keep his Patsy's-esque label. And amazingly, he found another law firm that would go along with the ruse. It backfired on the lawyers spectacularly.

Brija hired another law firm, Pennie & Edmonds. The new firm was fully aware of the false statements in the affidavit. They even asked Brija about them. He continued to lie, insisting that his sauce label was created in 1993 or 1994. When asked about the mismatched bar code on the 1993 label, Brija said he made a mistake and attached a 1999 label to the affidavit instead of the 1993 label. When asked about the invoices with an area code that did not exist in 1993, Brija threw his printing firm—Keller Label & Ticket Company—under the bus, claiming that the guy at Keller "took it upon himself to fabricate the records because he no longer had his records from 1993, and he did not tell this to Mr. Brija." Brija even produced a signed statement to that effect from Keller's account representative, Richard Mazzella.

Pennie & Edmonds contacted Mazzella's lawyer, who said that Mazzella didn't want to get involved, and that the signed statement was done without conferring with a lawyer. If Mazzella were subpoenaed, the lawyer added, "he would testify that he had not even done business with the defendants in 1993." So, Pennie & Edmonds was on notice that Brija was probably still lying, and that Mazzella wasn't willing to stand by his written statement. It was likely false too.

Here again, many students before coming to law school assume that the lawyer's job is to argue, argue, argue and win, win, win. Not so. Lawyers have to be measured and take their licks. Pennie & Edmonds hadn't learned that lesson yet.

Despite its lying client, Pennie & Edmonds filed papers with the court in support of Brija's claim that his labels were legitimate, attaching a new affidavit by Brija that made bogus excuses for the discrepancies in the facts.

The court saw through this maneuver, entered another ruling for Patsy's, and sanctioned Pennie & Edmonds for submitting another false affidavit. The court wrote: "[C]ounsel overlooks the irrefutable evidence that Brija's current story concerning an earlier label which he now claims he used in 1993 is as false as his claim that the current label had been in use since 1993." Moreover, the court added, the new label "contains on its face clear evidence that what Brija says is not true." As the court explained, the law doesn't allow lawyers to submit to the court "false statements of fact simply because a witness was willing to sign an affidavit that any reasonable lawyer would recognize as perjury." Under the procedural rules that govern federal courts, lawyers can be fined or disciplined for filing facts or law that are flatly wrong. In the Pennie & Edmonds case, the court published its opinion knowing that it would embarrass the law firm, which otherwise had a "fine reputation," and therefore deter it from doing something like that again.

The court explained what was likely going on behind the scenes at the law firm:

> The Court is familiar enough with large law firm practice in New York to know that this is a typical large law firm situation in which a client is introduced to the firm by one partner but the litigation is handled by another. The Court is also aware of the substantial economic benefits that flow to "finders," the partners who find the clients, and the pressure to please the client that is felt by the "minders," the lawyers that actually do the client's work. Thus, the litigating partner in this case no doubt felt an obligation to his partners not to jeopardize the firm's relationship with the client by telling the client that the client's factual statements were not credible in light of all of the contrary evidence.

The client, in other words, wasn't willing or ready to accept Step 5 of the B-I-C-A-T framework after his first set of lawyers refused to continue to represent him—that is, the hard reality that he was going to lose the trademark case, that his restaurant would likely have to pay Patsy's some money in addition to halting use of the labels, and that the best course of action would be to try to strike a settlement with Patsy's rather than risk an adverse judgment by the court. The second law firm wasn't willing to tell him the hard truth, either.

Of course, the difference between Patsy's case and regular life is that no judge is overseeing our decision-making with the reality check of an adverse judgment. Yet if we adhere—like Brija—to black-and-white thinking and the belief that the only way to "win" is to have things work out one way, we might feel angry or cheated or dissatisfied however the dispute resolves. But life, like law, is mostly gray. There is a 100% chance that we will face big decisions that require trade-offs. If we accept from the get-go that we will have to tolerate something less than a black or white outcome (whichever is our preference) and instead hold on to our values in evaluating the options, then the decision will "sit" better in our lives overall. We will have more "buy-in," or willingness to actively support the decision—even if it fell short in important respects.

The Patsy's case also brings forth another theme of this chapter: hiring a lawyer. To be sure, Brija was on a mission to have his false narrative vindicated in court—an impossibility, because courts are bound by rules of evidence and procedure (recall what we learned about this under Step 3, i.e., the knowledge-collection part of the framework). But Brija also apparently chose a lawyer whom he believed would do his bidding no matter what, due to a prior business relationship with the firm. This arrogance came back to haunt him when he faced the judge the second time around. The outcome of the trademark ruling might have been different had he gotten a steely-eyed assessment by a law firm that he'd lose because he lied the first time, his lie was on the record, and the court was not going to look kindly at another cynical bite at the apple.

When you are looking to hire a lawyer, be aware that you might not like the advice you ultimately hear. If you have a gripe with your employer, for example, on the belief that you were overlooked for a promotion because of your age, a lawyer might tell you that there's no case there. This is very different from being told that you weren't harmed. The question is whether you were harmed in a way that could produce a remedy in court. To prove discrimination based on age, you'd have to show that you were similarly situated to another employee (e.g., in terms of workload, seniority, education, performance reviews), but you didn't get the promotion. The younger person did. And the only difference between you was your relative age. If the lawyer doesn't see facts that fit this particular narrative, there's likely no case—even if, in fairness, you should have gotten the promotion. This kind of advice can be hard to hear. Step 5 prepares you for it.

Let's take a step back for a moment and review what kinds of matters might be worth hiring a lawyer for.

Criminal Defense. If you are arrested or, worse, indicted for an alleged crime, you will likely need a lawyer. The Sixth Amendment to the U.S. Constitution requires the "assistance of counsel" for an accused "in all criminal prosecutions." But that doesn't mean a guaranteed right to counsel for free. In 1963, the Supreme Court held in *Gideon v. Wainwright* that criminal defendants who cannot afford a lawyer are entitled to one paid for by the government. These public defense lawyers typically have very heavy caseloads and may not have the bandwidth to provide the kind of quality representation that a privately paid lawyer can provide. The law varies, as well, regarding what stage in the criminal justice process a court-appointed lawyer kicks in. In federal court and in most state courts, for example, there is no right to counsel for a bail hearing. Even if you need a lawyer for that, it's sadly not within every person's reach.

In the criminal justice system, a lawyer is important for several reasons, including making sure that you don't waive any of your constitutional and procedural rights, explaining the steps in the process, potentially negotiating a plea deal or dismissal of the charges against you, and building a defense for trial if it comes to that. Like many aspects of American life, access to good lawyers is an advantage of people with high incomes. With more resources, lawyers can dig more deeply into the facts in your defense.

Family Law. As you probably gathered by now, it is my view that avoiding lawyers in divorce cases is probably optimal. As in my case, lawyers can enhance acrimony—not lessen it—depending on the style of the counsel you hire. But in some states, as mentioned earlier, the same lawyer cannot represent both people in a divorce, even if all that lawyer does is memorialize a settlement agreement in writing. So, if your partner has a lawyer, you might decide you need one too, in order to finalize things.

If you want to avoid lawyers, do an internet search and click on the website for your state's family court—the forms that you need to file to do a divorce on your own are usually online, and court personnel can often be helpful with questions. The trick is getting to a place under Step 5 of the B-I-C-A-T framework where both parties realize that litigation is more costly than it's worth. Working through Steps 1 through 4—for each or both of you—could help get you to that place.

Trust and Estate Law. In the chapter on health care decisions, we reviewed the kinds of documents that are worth having in hand in the event of a serious medical emergency or death. These include a health care proxy or health care power of attorney in addition to a traditional power of attorney, as well as a document making clear what you want to happen if you are put on life support, for example. These kinds of documents can avoid family strife and anxiety while ensuring that your own wishes are honored. Keep in mind, too, that if you have a child eighteen years or older, you should have these documents executed for your child—just because you are the parent will not give you legal authority to make health decisions for your child once they reach a certain age. As mentioned before, there are online websites that allow you to complete and file these documents yourself, depending on the laws of the state in which you reside.

Litigation. When you are sued, it's best to hire a lawyer to defend you. If you want to sue someone else, a lawyer helps too. What I tell my students is that if the case involves Judge Judy–type damages—the kinds that wind up on the TV show of the same name—then proceeding without a lawyer, or "pro se," is okay. Imagine your neighbor knocks down your one-of-a-kind bird feeder, that costs $350 to replace. That's a Judge Judy case. You can probably handle it on your own, without a law degree. But if your catering business is sued for sexual harassment by an employee, you probably want to hire a lawyer because the stakes are much higher.

What about those billboards you see on the highway offering to represent you if you've been in a car accident? Well, many of those kinds of lawyers work on what's called a contingency fee. They only get paid if they win some sort of money judgment for you or persuade the party you are suing to give you a settlement payment. It may not cost you a dime. If they win the case for you, you pay them a percentage of the money they win for you. That amount is determined ahead of time. But those lawyers don't take those kinds of cases unless they are pretty sure that they will win. So, you might call the toll free number only to be turned down.

Other lawyers work exclusively on an hourly basis. In big cities, top lawyers may charge more than $1,000 an hour, plus the hourly time of their associates and paralegals. Litigation costs can quickly turn into the hundreds of thousands or even millions of dollars, and most of the time, you must pay your own fees—even if you win your case. American law doesn't shift the fees onto the losing party in most instances.

A third category of lawyers bills by the task—like drafting a will or doing the paperwork to close on the sale of a house. Even in those cases, however, if your matter is especially complex—like a will involving multiple businesses and millions of dollars—a lawyer will charge a higher rate or require an hourly billing arrangement. Even for hourly billing, moreover, many lawyers will require a retainer—say $5,000 up front—which they will put in an escrow account and draw from as they perform work for you. That way, they can be sure they get paid. And they are legally not allowed to dip into the account except in payment of your attorneys' fees.

Finally, some lawyers work pro bono—or for free—in areas other than criminal law. It is difficult to secure this kind of representation, but many law schools across the country have what are called "legal aid clinics" in which law students represent primarily low-income clients on issues from family law to social security and disability filings. There are many non-profit organizations of lawyers that specialize in certain actions, such as protecting the environment or civil rights. On this topic too, however, there are specialties. Some places represent individual clients to resolve their personal issues with a landlord, for example. Others focus on what's called "impact litigation"—they file lawsuits aimed at changing the law across the country on a big issue like voting rights.

One summer when I was in law school, I worked at an organization in Oakland, California, that did both impact litigation and individual representation on behalf of Native Americans living in California. I wrote a brief in a lawsuit aimed at enabling a prison inmate to secure an eagle feather for a religious ceremony and another for a prisoner who didn't want to cut his hair out of respect for his culture. Eagles are endangered species, so the feathers are hard to obtain. A favorable ruling in those cases could have affected Native Americans across the country. (I was in law school before the case was resolved, so I don't know how it ultimately turned out.) But we also conducted small clinics across the state that helped Native populations manage tricky red tape when it came to obtaining government benefits and other matters. If you are looking for a pro bono lawyer, be aware that you probably want someone who does the latter kind of pro bono work—that is, helping individuals with personal issues rather than filing lawsuits with the aim of bringing about widespread change.

Complex Business Filings. There are a range of matters that companies need lawyers for—from tax filings to structuring a business, from securities matters to contract drafting and negotiation, and from employment-related issues to bankruptcy. Hiring a good lawyer early in the process can avoid litigation and other problems later. It can be well worth the up-front expense. I teach a class in federal litigation procedure, which is one of the most important classes in law school. Why? Because any lawyer knows—whatever one's particular expertise—that litigation is always looming if things go wrong. Thus, every lawyer needs to understand how that system works.

Tolerate Conflicted Feelings

Let's apply Step 5 of the framework to the decision to hire a lawyer. Imagine that you are opening a neighborhood restaurant in a space that was previously occupied by a hair salon. There are other restaurants on the block, but the neighbors who reside just behind the alley butting up to the restaurant don't want another eating establishment close by. They claim that it will bring rats and they decide to do whatever they can to stop your business from opening.

You need to secure a liquor license for the restaurant, which requires that the neighborhood council hold a hearing for resident complaints. The hearing is raucous, and a couple of people are really angry. They convince enough members of the liquor board to hold off on the license until the next meeting, which is two months away. Meanwhile, you are paying rent on the space already, you've invested tens of thousands of dollars in the renovation, and you hired a staff to start in ten days. It is costing you money every single day that the opening is delayed. Do you hire a lawyer now?

Let's go through the various B-I-C-A-T steps so far. Under Step 1, the problem might be broken down as follows:

- Lost income from delays
- Cost of hiring a lawyer
- Other options for addressing the problem

Under Step 2, identifying values, you might list subjects like ensuring fairness, responsibility, reputation, and accountability. After all, each of these issues are important for a neighborhood restaurant—you've lived in that community for years and don't want to burn bridges. At the same time, you need to be accountable to your employees and your investors.

Next you name your aim: opening as quickly as possible, even if it means spending a little extra money to do so, and turning a profit. You ask around and get the name of a lawyer who specializes in the business of opening restaurants (there are people like that out there, but again, that does not necessarily mean they are good at what they do).

Step 3 is to collect lots of knowledge. You go online and pull up the regulations that apply to new restaurants in your town, the criteria for obtaining a liquor license, and the names of the liquor board members. Then maybe you ask around to see if anyone knows any of those people—and maybe even knows the obstreperous neighbors. Perhaps you can make the case to one or more of those folks in person. It turns out your inquiry produces the name of a man who lives right behind the restaurant and is also on the board. You contact him, and he agrees to have coffee with you. He tells you he knows the people who are on the board and isn't optimistic that they will change their minds anytime soon. You leave empty-handed.

Step 4 is to pre-argue both sides of the issues for yourself. Delays are costing you money daily, but so will lawyers, with no guarantee that they will get your license for you more quickly. In addition, the liquor license doesn't necessarily preclude you from opening—you just can't serve alcohol. On the question of the cost of hiring a lawyer, the up-front expense could be significant. But on the other hand, it could pay off if you get the license quickly. You know that liquor sales are a major part of a sit-down restaurant's revenue and will be a big draw for customers. You did the numbers, and you can't survive and make a profit if you are only selling food, given your labor costs and other out-of-pocket expenses. The first few weeks of a restaurant are often the most vital for getting a foothold on the market, so you want to put your best foot forward on opening day—which means selling alcohol.

The last issue on your breakdown is whether you have other options. You tried to broker something on your own and it didn't move the needle. But there's no predicting whether a lawyer could do that for you, either. You could end up having spent significant sums only to wind up in no better position than you are now.

You look at your values and your aims and decide that

opening as quickly as possible and maximizing the possibility of making money with liquor sales is your primary aim, which could be served by hiring a lawyer. But because you care a lot about your reputation in the neighborhood—and you know it's central to the vitality of your business—you must be careful not to hire someone who is too aggressive. You want a lawyer who is effective, but not alienating.

This is a real-life story about someone I know. He did hire a lawyer, who reached out to the people who wanted to stop the restaurant and brokered a settlement. The tentative deal was that the restaurant owner would allow the neighbors to "police" the dumpster for violations of municipal law. If the restaurant violated those rules, then the neighbors could enforce them as a matter of contract law under the settlement. In other words, if there were rats in the alley, the neighbors could sue the owner for breach of their settlement contract as if they were deputized police officers. Yikes!

This suggestion was a big deal. Most of the time, it's the city that enforces its own regulations. If someone is parked in a no-parking zone, the government issues the ticket—not a private citizen. If a dumpster is smelly and overflowing, a neighbor has to call the city to get some sort of enforcement action. There is normally no right to go to court and enforce the law on behalf of the city. What the lawyer was proposing, therefore, was a significant gift to the neighbors at a big price to the client. At my recommendation as a friend, the restaurant owner turned it down.

In deciding whether to accept the lawyer's proposed settlement, the restaurant owner could have done well to look back to his aims: opening as quickly as possible and turning a profit. Although the settlement proposal might have served the first aim, it could have been rapidly eclipsed by losses on the second. It's entirely possible that the discontented neighbors would lodge incessant claims that the restaurant owner breached his contractual promise to abide by city regulations or risk a lawsuit. Defending against that kind of potentially endless litigation could quickly dry up whatever profits earlier liquor sales accumulated. He decided to wait for the next liquor board meeting, and ultimately got the license—without the ball and chain attached to the angry neighbors.

This might seem like a story designed to dissuade people from hiring lawyers. But that's not my intention. To be sure, the restaurant owner spent money on the lawyer, got his advice, and rejected it. But consider Step 5: Tolerating the fact that people will disagree with your choice—and that you might feel conflicted. The restaurant owner might have disappointed his lawyer. He certainly disappointed the already unhappy neighbors. He might have even disappointed his investors, who were anxious to get the place open. And he might have felt conflicted, too. But having gone through the careful B-I-C-A-T process, he can feel comfortable with the conflict. He knew that there was no "100% win" option. The problem didn't have a black or white solution. He gave some things up—an immediate opening with a liquor license and the money that would come with that—but wound up preserving deeper values and aims.

Of course, people make decisions like this every day without going through anything resembling a deliberate five-step process. That's fine—and often works well. Much of what is in this book might be second nature to you already; you just weren't aware of it. But if you are anything like me, there are times in life when the considerations, potential problems, and options surrounding a decision can seem overwhelming. You feel flooded, and don't know what to do next. Often, this is because you are focusing on resolving the ultimate decision—not the steps or process for getting there. The B-I-C-A-T method forces you to break things down into manageable chunks, dissolve some stress along the way, and hopefully arrive at a decision you can live with—even if somebody else might not think it the very "best" one.

STEP 5 CHECKLIST: TOLER-ATE THE FACT THAT PEOPLE WILL DISAGREE WITH YOUR CHOICE

✓ List your values and your aim.

✓ Which option aligns with those?

✓ List what you wanted that you didn't get.

✓ List what you did get that aligns with your values and aims. Feel good about that.

CONCLUSION

The B-I-C-A-T
Method Revisited

Now that we've gotten through the B-I-C-A-T framework, let's apply it to our opening hypothetical—the one about the slip-and-fall at Hotel Ooh La La. Recall that when faced with my basic "what to do about this scenario?" question posed around this hypothetical, law students almost always want to immediately sue the hotel. Perhaps it's because they're in law school, and lawyers are infamously known to file lots of lawsuits. But the students' response is also probably due to the natural human tendency to engage in quick, reactive decision-making. As discussed earlier in this book, quick decision-making can be extremely helpful and important; it's hardwired in the human brain. But because litigation is expensive, stressful, and risky, a knee-jerk decision is not what's called for in my opening hypothetical. Drawing that distinction around how lawyers think is precisely why I use this hypothetical year after year. Good lawyers think through issues very carefully before rendering an opinion and a strategy.

Here, again, is the framework:

1. **Break** the problem down.
2. **Identify** your values and your aim.
3. **Collect** lots of knowledge.
4. **Argue** both sides of each point.
5. **Tolerate** the fact that people will disagree with your choice—and that you might feel conflicted.

So, imagine that you are the law student on vacation in my opening hypothetical. Imagine too that after the incident you manage to get to the emergency room and leave with a cast on your foot. You don't have health insurance, so the visit costs you $850, including x-rays. You put it on a credit card. Plus, you are told that you must see an orthopedist in a week, which will mean more x-rays and follow-up visits. You estimate that your medical bills could run you around $2,500. If the ankle doesn't heal properly, you could need physical therapy or even surgery—so that number could climb significantly.

Meanwhile, you are due to begin law school in a few weeks, and your third-floor apartment that you signed a lease for does not have an elevator. You worry that the ankle will affect your ability to succeed in school—both because of the psychological and emotional stress as well as the basics of getting to and from class with a broken ankle. If you wind up having to postpone your law school start date due to the injury, it could affect your financial aid and a host of other concerns. Moreover, you are just angry that Hotel Ooh La La lured you there with what turned out to be a bogus vacation package. You want justice. What do you do?

Step 1 of the B-I-C-A-T framework breaks the problem down. It might look something like this:

- Payment of out-of-pocket medical costs
- Reimbursement for pain, suffering, and inconvenience
- Interference with legal education
- Retaining counsel
- Chances of success

Step 2 is to identify your values and name your aim. This one is critical, as litigation could throw you off course in terms of your education even if it winds up making you financially whole. Here's a list of possible values:

- Fairness and justice
- Financial security
- Psychological and physical wellness
- Efficiency
- Adhering to educational goals

From this list, you next identify which is the *most* important— the one or two that you are willing to sideline other values for. For the sake of argument, let's assume that you pick the last one— adhering to your educational goals. As a secondary value, you might choose financial security, because the unidentified medical costs could negatively affect your primary aim: getting your law degree as efficiently and effectively as possible.

Step 3 is to collect lots of knowledge—both regarding the

facts and the law. Hopefully, a visit with an orthopedist will help you get more information about the longer-term implications for your ankle. You might call the law school and find out what kind of help is available if you are not fully mobile the first few weeks of school. After all, there are laws that require reasonable accommodations for disabilities. As for the law governing your case against the hotel, you might reach out to your personal and professional network for the name of a personal injury lawyer—or even look for one online and get a free consultation regarding the chances of success for your claim. You should also read the fine print of whatever documents you signed when you made your reservation and checked into the hotel—they could contain stipulations regarding the hotel's liability and how claims are processed (sometimes you are forced to go to arbitration or mediation without even realizing that's what you agreed to when you signed the paperwork at check-in). Finally, you might also ask anyone else you know who might have been at that hotel on the date of your injuries for photos or other information about the conditions of the pool.

Step 4 is to map out arguments for both sides of each point contained in the breakdown of issues under Step 1. For this step, the bottom-line question is really whether to pursue some sort of formal process against the hotel or just move on. This is tricky. There are several decisions that a lawyer would have to make before filing a lawsuit—including where to file it. If you can file in your home state, that would be great for you—but it might not legally work against Hotel Ooh La La. Trekking to Las Vegas to pursue your claim might make it not worth it. Moreover, much will depend on the law that applies to your case—Nevada law is not identical to other states' laws when it comes to tort liability. You might not be able to get complete information on these legal nuances before you decide on what to do.

If you do nothing, however, Hotel Ooh La La will "get away with" its shady advertising tactics—potentially harming other future law students—as well as its unsafe pool environment. This really bothers you. At a minimum, you need help with medical costs from Hotel Ooh La La. And if the law allows recovery for your pain and suffering (versus just reimbursement for out-of-pocket medical costs), you could get extra money to help with law school expenses.

Under Step 5, let's assume you decide to forgo litigation and instead write a letter asking Hotel Ooh La La to reimburse you for your medical costs. You might even hire a lawyer to write the letter on law firm letterhead, costing you a few hundred bucks, to maximize the chance that the hotel will respond. But the hotel might not take the bait. Maybe this is par for the course, and the hotel knows that law students can't afford lawsuits—it keeps up the bad practices because they are profitable. You might ultimately be out the money on health care, the time it took to make this decision, and the emotional energy spent on reconciling that Hotel Ooh La La isn't going to meet with justice this time. But having gone through the entire B-I-C-A-T framework, perhaps you can go off to law school knowing that you thought through the issue so thoroughly that you can feel okay about the outcome, however imperfect.

I hope it's evident by now that even this basic hypothetical is not as clear-cut as it seems, as my law students quickly come to re-alize on their first day of law school. Indeed, the human tendency to see things in black and white cannot be overstated. Nor can its adverse effects be underestimated—particularly these days when polarization has infected everything from politics to health care. But this isn't new. For centuries, bifurcated categorizations have permeated literature and popular culture. Stories ranging from *Cinderella* to *The Lord of the Rings* to *Game of Thrones* routinely involve depictions of good versus evil, villains versus saints. The appeal of these stories is obvious. By associating ourselves with the do-gooder "side," we feel good about ourselves. In our own lives, putting an issue or a person in a pre-defined box helps dif-fuse anxiety too. The world seems clear and easily defined.

Demonizing and marginalizing the other side can entail a high price, though—not only for the other party, but also for ourselves. It restricts our ability to think through thorny, nu-anced problems. We miss things that could be important, if not vital. It could even leave us feeling abandoned when the white knight in our lives turns dark—with no grayscale, there's hardly a third option for hanging on to a relationship, even if it's the best thing for us in the long run.

Lawyers are not usually psychologists, of course. But we do know a few things about how to bring a dispute to a resolution. The process is not always pretty, and lawyers don't always add value, quiet tempers, or maximize efficiency. Still, the profession persists. The first law school in the United States—now the Wil-liam & Mary Law School in Williamsburg, Virginia—accepted its first student in 1779. In the 243 years since, we've seen technological advances that include electricity, automobiles, airplanes, rockets to the moon, computers, and smartphones. Some experts believe that artificial intelligence could one day become "billions of times smarter" than humans, potentially merging with the human brain. Whether lawyers will one day likewise become redundant or useless is hard to say. But I'll believe it only when I see it.

For now, there is no computer or app out there that can simulate the assistance of legal counsel—even though thousands of laws are available in full text in our pockets. By simply typing or dictating a search into our smartphones, the law on virtually any subject pops up. No more needing to go to libraries—let alone a dusty legal one. If we need legal translations, dictionaries and explainers are readily available online too. Why isn't the internet enough to displace lawyers? Because American law schools are still in the business of teaching people *how* to think—not *what* to think. It's a valuable skill, and one that only an elite and privileged percentage of people have access to through a formal J.D. program. Computers cannot yet provide it.

The purpose of this book is to bring a measure of that valuable skill—the *how* to think better part of legal education—to regular people, with five easy steps. My hope is to guide readers in bringing a bit of order to the chaos that we all feel at times. By shifting focus to the *questions*—like lawyers do—and away from defending pre-determined *conclusions*, perhaps we can each make a tiny difference in the broader public good, as well.

My challenge to every reader is simple: Change your mind about something today. Anything. It could be your dislike for pickles. Or your preference to Sean Connery's James Bond over Daniel Craig's. Or your views on hot-button political or religious topics. Pick something and apply B-I-C-A-T to it. As with law students, the more you do it, the more second nature it will become. By practicing the art of lawyering—which looks for nuances on the other side of the coin, not just our own—I believe we can all move closer to one another, bit by bit.

Citations

INTRODUCTION

On legal reasoning generally: https://codolc.com/books/Thinking_Like
_a_Lawyer.pdf

On medical professionals and decision-making: https://www.npr.org
/templates/story/story.php?storyId=8892053

On computer simulation of medical diagnosis: https://www.nature.com
/articles/s41598-018-20826-y

On the history of decision-making: https://hbr.org/2006/01/a-brief-
history-of-decision-making

On Asch conformity experiment: https://www.verywellmind.com/the
-asch-conformity-experiments-2794996

On Trump's gut: https://www.cnn.com/2018/11/27/politics/washington
-post-trump-gut/index.html

On George Soros: https://www.irishtimes.com/business/personal-finance
/buy-bubbles-bet-big-and-backache-soros-s-secrets-1.1893639

On brain chemistry: https://www.smashingmagazine.com/2019/02/human
-decision-making

On belief bias: https://www.frontiersin.org/articles/10.3389/fpsyg.2019.02940
/full; https://www.forbes.com/sites/stephaniesarkis/2019/05/26/emotions-over
ruling-logic-how-belief-bias-alters-your-decisions/#3b523af67c56

On hindsight bias: https://examples.yourdictionary.com/examples-of-hindsight -bias.html

On omission bias: https://www.sas.upenn.edu/~baron/papers.htm/sq.html

On confirmation bias: https://www.verywellmind.com/what-is-a-confirmation -bias-2795024

On escalation of commitment: https://hbr.org/1987/03/knowing-when-to -pull-the-plug

On heuristics and problem-solving strategies: http://www.inquiriesjournal .com/articles/180/decision-making-factors-that-influence-decision -making-heuristics-used-and-decision-outcomes

CHAPTER 1

On the body's response to stress: https://www.mayoclinic.org/healthy -lifestyle/stress-management/in-depth/stress/art-20046037; https://www.ncbi .nlm.nih.gov/pmc/articles/PMC4263906

Pennoyer v. Neff, 95 U.S. 714 (1878). Wendy Purdue, "Sin, Scandal and Substantive Due Process: Personal Jurisdiction and Pennoyer Reconsidered," 62 *Wash. L. Rev.* 479 (1987)

On Oregon: Howard M. Corning, ed., *Dictionary of Oregon History* (Binford & Mort 1989); Paul Frymer, *Building an American Empire: The Era of Territorial and Political Expansion* (Princeton University Press 2017); https://www.oregonencyclopedia.org/articles/oregon_donation_land _act/#.YAS04C2cZTY

On excitement response: https://blog.hubspot.com/marketing/psychology -of-excitement

On website developers: https://www.bls.gov/ooh/computer-and-information -technology/web-developers.htm#tab-5

On sleep: https://www.smithsonianmag.com/science-nature/experiments -show-we-really-can-learn-while-we-sleep-141518869

CHAPTER 2

On family life cycle: https://www.consumerpsychologist.com/cb_Family _Decision_Making.html

On family decision-making research: https://www.acrwebsite.org/volumes /6976/volumes/v16/NA-16

On three-person parenting: https://www.theatlantic.com/family/archive /2020/09/how-build-three-parent-family-david-jay/616421

On definition of "Law": https://www.dictionary.com/browse/law?s=t

On values: https://www.researchgate.net/publication/280231030_Values _Psychological_Perspectives

Scott v. Harris, 550 U.S. 372 (2007). Streaming video: https://archive.org /details/opinion_video2

On Maslow: https://www.simplypsychology.org/maslow.html

On yin and yang: https://www.jordanbpeterson.com/podcast/s3-e2 -biblical-series-genesis-1-chaos-order/

CHAPTER 3

On juries: https://www.britannica.com/topic/jury

On big data statistics: https://www.sciencefocus.com/future-technology /how-much-data-is-on-the-internet/; https://info.cobaltiron.com/blog/petabyte -how-much-information-could-it-actually-hold

On the Apollo missions' computer: https://www.ibm.com/ibm/history/ ibm100/us/en/icons/apollo/breakthroughs/; https://astronomy.com/news /2019/05/apollo-computers-when-ibm-engineers-gave-rockets-a-brain

On life expectancy: https://ourworldindata.org/life-expectancy

On confirmation bias: https://www.verywellmind.com/cognitive-biases -distort-thinking-2794763; https://examples.yourdictionary.com/confirmation -bias-examples-in-real-life.html

On death-row exonerations: https://www.aclu.org/other/dna-testing-and -death-penalty

Hickman v. Taylor, 329 U.S. 495 (1947); 170 F.2d 327 (3d Cir. 1948)

On benefits of service: https://www.mentalfloss.com/article/71964/7 -scientific-benefits-helping-others

On Rotary clubs: https://www.rotary.org/en/about-rotary

On journalists' code of ethics: https://www.spj.org/ethicscode.asp

On the FCC's fairness doctrine: https://www.britannica.com/topic/Fairness-Doctrine

Communications Decency Act of 1996, 47 U.S.C. § 230

On the debate over Section 230: https://www.cfr.org/in-brief/trump-and-section-230-what-know

On big data surveillance: https://www.nytimes.com/2021/01/29/opinion/sunday/facebook-surveillance-society-technology.html

On running for office: https://www.kiplinger.com/article/business/t043-c000-s002-how-to-run-for-local-office.html

CHAPTER 4

On voter statistics on health care as a priority: https://www.kff.org/report-section/kff-health-tracking-poll-early-april-2020-the-impact-of-coronavirus-on-life-in-america-politics-findings

CDC Statistics: https://www.cdc.gov/nchs/products/databriefs/db395.htm

On health care proxy and other documents: https://www.success.com/3-important-health-care-decisions-to-consider

On the Americans with Disabilities Act of 1990: https://www.dol.gov/general/topic/disability/ada

Evening Star Newspaper Company v. Kemp, 533 F.2d 1224 (D.C. Cir. 1976)

The ranger hypothetical is borrowed from Funk, Shapiro, and Weaver's *Administrative Procedure and Practice: A Contemporary Approach*, Revised 6th Edition

On cataract surgery: https://www.mayoclinic.org/tests-procedures/cataract-surgery/about/pac-20384765

On botched plastic surgery: http://www.thewealthydentist.com/blog/566/dentist-botches-breast-surgery

On subconscious information processing: https://www.healthline.com

/health-news/let-your-brain-process-decisions-subconsciously#How-You
-Subconsciously-Decide

On HIPAA: https://www.hhs.gov/hipaa/for-individuals/guidance-materials
-for-consumers/index.html

CHAPTER 5

On black-and-white thinking: https://www.talkspace.com/blog/black
-white-thinking-ways-poisons-your-perspective

Patsy's Brand, Inc. v. I.O.B. Realty, Inc., 2002 WL 59434 (S.D.N.Y. Jan. 16,
2002), *vacated* sub nom. *In re Pennie & Edmonds LLP*, 323 F.3d 86 (2d Cir.
2003)

Gideon v. Wainwright, 372 U.S. 335 (1963)

CONCLUSION

On the first American law school: https://scholarship.law.wm.edu/timeline

On artificial intelligence: https://www.cnbc.com/2018/02/13/a-i-will-be
-billions-of-times-smarter-than-humans-man-and-machine-need-to
-merge.html

Acknowledgments

Thanks again to my wonderful editor, Sara Nelson, and my agent, Paul Fedorko, whose enthusiasm and support for my work are nothing short of humbling. Thanks too to my sister Colleen James, and my former student and friend Raquel Bowings, for reviewing prior drafts and offering candid and vital feedback. It's impossible to acknowledge all the colleagues, mentors, teachers, judges, opposing counsel, and students whose influence is reflected in the pages of this book, which represents many years of honing the craft of teaching as it relates to essential questions of civics and human communication. I hope the spirit of fostering understanding and tolerance comes through, and that it will be shared by many, with many, and for many years to come.

Acknowledgments

About the Author

Kim Wehle is a tenured professor of law at the University of Baltimore School of Law, where she teaches and writes on the constitutional separation of powers, administrative law, and civil procedure. She was formerly an assistant United States attorney and an associate independent counsel in the Whitewater investigation. Professor Wehle is also a legal expert, analyst, and commentator for numerous media outlets, including CNN, CBS News, BBC, NPR, and MSNBC, and is an opinion writer for *The Atlantic, Politico, The Bulwark*, and *The Hill*. She hosts *#SimplePolitics with Kim Wehle* on Instagram and YouTube. She lives in Chevy Chase, Maryland, with her children. Follow her on Twitter: @kimwehle.

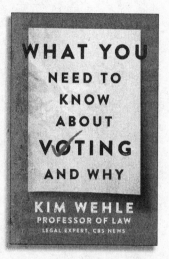
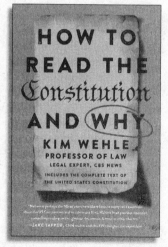